Heart-Felt
Holidays

Heart-Felt Holidays

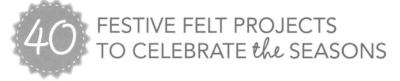

40 FESTIVE FELT PROJECTS
TO CELEBRATE *the* SEASONS

KATHY SHELDON & AMANDA CARESTIO

LARK CRAFTS

Asheville

Book Packager
KATHY SHELDON

Art Director
SUSAN WASINGER

Art Assistant
KAY HOLMES STAFFORD

Illustrator
ORRIN LUNDGREN

Photographer
SUSAN WASINGER

Cover Designer
SUSAN WASINGER

LARK CRAFTS

An Imprint of Sterling Publishing
387 Park Avenue South
New York, NY 10016

If you have questions or comments about
this book, please visit: larkcrafts.com

Library of Congress Cataloging-in-Publication Data

Sheldon, Kathy
  Heart-felt holidays : 40 festive felt projects to celebrate the seasons / Kathy Sheldon & Amanda Carestio. --1st ed.
     p. cm.
  Includes index.
  ISBN 978-1-4547-0281-8
  1. Holiday decorations. 2. Felt work. I. Carestio, Amanda. II. Title.
  TT900.C4.S52 2012
  746'.0463--dc23

                              2011027335

10 9 8 7 6 5 4 3 2 1

First Edition

Published by Lark Crafts
An Imprint of Sterling Publishing Co., Inc.
387 Park Avenue South, New York, NY 10016

Text © 2012, Kathy Sheldon
Photography © 2012, Lark Crafts, an Imprint of Sterling Publishing Co., Inc., unless otherwise specified
Photographs pages 36 and 37 © 2012, Dana Willard
Illustrations © 2012, Lark Crafts, an Imprint of Sterling Publishing Co., Inc., unless otherwise specified

Distributed in Canada by Sterling Publishing,
c/o Canadian Manda Group, 165 Dufferin Street
Toronto, Ontario, Canada M6K 3H6

Distributed in the United Kingdom by GMC Distribution Services,
Castle Place, 166 High Street, Lewes, East Sussex, England BN7 1XU

Distributed in Australia by Capricorn Link (Australia) Pty Ltd.,
P.O. Box 704, Windsor, NSW 2756 Australia

Manufactured in China

ISBN 13: 978-1-4547-0281-8

For information about custom editions, special sales, and premium and corporate purchases,
please contact Sterling Special Sales Department at 800-805-5489 or specialsales@sterlingpub.com.

Requests for information about desk and examination copies available to college and university professors must be
submitted to academic@larkbooks.com. Our complete policy can be found at www.larkcrafts.com.

Contents

Introduction   PAGE 6

Felt Basics   PAGE 7

Holiday Projects

Cheers! Banner   14   Rockets' Red Glare   64
No-Sew Wine Bags   16   July 4th Bunting   66
I Have a Dream Garland   20   Yo Ho Ho Pirate Parrot   68
Chinese Luck Lantern   22   Bat Costume   72
Seeing Shadows Phone Case   24   Halloweenie Bag   75
Mushroom Love Brooch   26   Great Mini Pumpkins   78
Blooming Valentines   28   (Pumpkin) Pie in the Sky   80
Heart Baubles   30   Autumn Leaves Coasters   82
Leprechaun Finger Puppet   32   Autumn Leaves Table Runner   84
Bunny Bunting   36   Happy Hanukkah Mice   87
Bunny Pal   38   Christmas Ornaments   90
Easter Egg Tree Ornaments   42   Mistletoe Kissing Ball   92
Earth Day Leaf Garlands   44   Merry Little Bowling Elves   94
April Showers   46   Kinara Felt Board   97
May Day Flowers Garland   48
Apple for Teacher Brooch   50   Celebration Projects
Piñata Ornaments   52   Happy Birthday Crown   100
Lavender Tea Bag Sachets   54   Cake Toppers   103
Early Bird Pillow   56   Toadstool Gift Bag   106
Felty Family Portraits   59   Flutterby Mobile   108
Manly Moustaches   62   Soft Baby Booties   110

Templates   PAGE 112

About the Designers   PAGE 129

Acknowledgments & About the Authors   PAGE 131

Index   PAGE 132

Introduction

HOW COME THOSE EXACT TIMES OF THE YEAR THAT WE SET ASIDE FOR having fun—holidays and special occasions—are also when we're so busy it's hard to relax and enjoy ourselves? When we put together *Fa la la la Felt*, our first book of Christmas decorations, we realized two things: A whole lot of awesome designers are working with felt these days, and felt is incredibly easy to stitch into fresh, adorable decorations. We couldn't wait to see what we'd end up with if we invited this talented group of designers to combine felt with holidays and celebrations like Valentine's Day, Halloween, and birthdays. We weren't disappointed, and you won't be either.

Fabulous fray-free felt (try saying that three times fast) is the fabric to reach for when you want to celebrate with homemade style and still have time to hide the Easter eggs or make the sweet potato casserole for Thanksgiving. This isn't the standard stuff your first grade teacher kept on the shelf above the finger paints. Felt varies wildly in both colors and content these days, from subtle heathered wool felt to screaming lime green felt made from recycled plastic bottles. So whether your take on a holiday calls for sweet, sassy, playful, or sophisticated, there's a felt out there that's perfect and longing to be turned into a festive bunting, an elegant table runner, or a happy birthday crown.

We've got your whole year covered! Quick, jump to page 22 and take a look at Aimee Ray's Chinese Luck Lantern to see how felt can get three-dimensional. Check out Cathy Gaubert's wee Leprechaun Finger Puppet on page 32 for St. Patrick's Day. And if you need a thoughtful gift for a baby shower, consider Laura Howard's sweet Flutterby Mobile on page 108. We've also included a few nontraditional holidays with projects like a thoughtful Apple Brooch for Teacher Appreciation Day (page 50) and a colorful parrot for (our personal favorite holiday) Talk Like a Pirate Day.

Of course, many of these decorations are appropriate for any season. The colorful flower garland on page 48 and the cheerful bird pillow on page 56 have "leave it out all year" appeal. You can adapt the Happy Hanukkah Mice on page 87 for any holiday. And we haven't left out Christmas. Ellen Luckett Baker's endearing Bowling Elves (page 94) are going to be awfully hard to pack away in the attic when January comes around. We hope this book brings you creative inspiration throughout the year, perhaps introduces you to a new holiday, and most of all, reminds you that special occasions don't need to be about fussing or perfection, but about sharing time with those you love in happy, homemade, and heart-FELT ways!

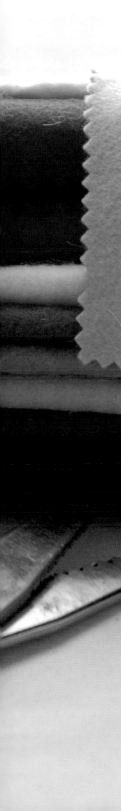

Felt Basics

When we say "basics," we mean it. Simplicity is part of the joy of working with felt, and even beginning sewers are likely to have and know most of what's needed to make the projects in this book. A quick trip to a fabric or craft store (who's not up for that?) should take care of any felt, embroidery thread, or other embellishments you don't already have on hand. Of course, you don't even need to leave your house to shop—a huge selection of felt and sewing supplies is available online. Check the list in the Basic Sewing Kit (page 9), and then skim the What You Need list before starting any project in the book. Most of the materials, tools, and techniques used are covered in this section, and you'll find templates in the back of the book. If you're the impatient sort who likes to jump right in and start crafting, you can skip this whole section, choose a project, and start making—then come back if you get stuck. That's what we'd do.

Basic Materials

FELT

Felt has become super popular recently for a reason—it's easy to cut, sew, and embellish and is beloved by crafters because it doesn't fray. All sorts of, well, let's face it, boring things that you have to do with fabric, you don't have to do with felt, leaving you more time for the fun parts of sewing!

The range of luscious colors and types of felt available is enough to make your head spin. You can find hand-dyed wool felt, wool/rayon felt, 100 percent acrylic felt, eco felt made from post-consumer recycled plastic bottles, and even felt made from bamboo and rayon. It comes in cut sheets or as yardage and in both solid colors and patterns. You can even buy stiffened felt sheets that hold their shape better than regular felt. And hey, we're talking about celebrating here: If your crafting motto is "too much ain't enough," we hear

that stiffened felt sheets embedded with glitter can be found! Purchase felt in fabric stores, craft stores, or online. A few of the projects in this book also call for felted material (fabric from wool items that have been purposely shrunk). See the sidebar on page 8 for simple felting instructions. In most cases, you can use whichever type of felt you prefer or happen to have on hand, but it's worth taking a look at the various kinds to see how they differ.

WOOL FELT One hundred percent wool is the thickest felt. It's the sturdiest, it hides needle holes and seams the best, and won't open up at the stitch holes when you stuff projects. You can dye wool felt or purchase it in beautiful and subtle hand-dyed colors. It won't tear apart or pill the way acrylic felt often does. Also, wool felt is less flammable than acrylic felt. But you can't machine wash or dry wool felt, it's more expensive than acrylic felt, and it's harder to find at your local big box craft store (you can, however, find plenty of wool felt online).

WOOL/RAYON FELT Wool/rayon felt is very similar to 100 percent wool felt. The addition of rayon makes the felt more flexible, so it's easier to sew and drapes a little better than pure wool felt. Wool/rayon felt costs less than wool felt but more than acrylic felt.

Creating Felted Fabric

A few of the projects in this book call for felted fabric. (You can always use another kind of felt instead—it just won't look quite the same.) Making felted fabric is easy; in fact, you've probably done it before when you've accidentally put a wool sweater through a laundry cycle. Here's how to do it on purpose:

1 Start with a 100 percent wool garment. Crafters typically use wool sweaters, but wool slacks, blazers, and winter coats also create beautiful felted fabric (take a look at Lisa Jordan's Autumn Leaves Coasters on page 82).

2 Remove any liners, zippers, buttons, etc., from your item, and then place it in a zippered lingerie bag or a pillow protector (to prevent wet lint from clogging up your washing machine).

3 Set your washer to the hot wash/cold rinse cycle, and use the lowest water level setting and the longest cycle. Add about one tablespoon of mild dish soap or wool wash.

4 If the material shrinks as desired, hang it to dry. If you want more shrinkage, wash it again and then dry it in your dryer. The end result should be soft felted fabric that won't ravel when cut. Use a sweater shaver to de-fuzz it and a steam iron to remove any wrinkles.

ACRYLIC FELT Acrylic felt is made by pressing tiny acrylic fibers until they interlock into a mat of material. Its benefits are that it's inexpensive, widely available, fade resistant, and you can machine wash and dry it. But acrylic felt is usually thinner—and therefore more transparent—than wool felt. It also stretches out of shape more easily, tends to gape and open up at stitch holes (especially in stuffed projects), and gets fuzzy if handled a lot.

ECO FELT Made from post-consumer plastic bottles, eco felt shares almost all of acrylic felt's characteristics, but it is, of course, reusing something that might otherwise clog the landfills. One added benefit of acrylic and eco felt is that people who are allergic to wool or are averse to using products that come from animals prefer them.

BAMBOO FELT New on the scene is bamboo felt. Super soft, bamboo felt is typically 50 percent bamboo and 50 percent rayon. This makes it a natural, renewable material that is also vegan. Your best place to find bamboo felt at this point is online.

THREAD AND FLOSS

When it comes to thread, spend a little bit more and get the good stuff. Buy a quality polyester, cotton/polyester blend, or all-cotton thread for machine and hand stitching. It will make sewing much easier and give you strong seams that will stay strong. For decorative embroidery stitches, your best bet is embroidery floss, available in just about every shade of every color you can imagine at craft and fabric stores. See page (11) for illustrations of all the stitches used in this book.

STUFFING

If our project instructions tell you to stuff it, you can use polyester fiberfill, cotton batting, wool roving, or even sewing scraps. The Lavender Tea Bag Sachets (page 54) call for dried lavender inside—heavenly.

EMBELLISHMENTS

Okay, we admit it: We love to shop for things like buttons, ribbon, and rickrack. Embellishments usually don't cost much and they are just so darn cute. Look through the projects you want to make, and note the trimmings you'll need, such as embroidery floss or ribbon. Of course, part of the fun of creating is doing your own thing, so feel free to think of the embellishments listed as suggestions and substitute freely.

Basic Tools

You don't need a lot of tools to make the projects in this book. Many can be sewn by hand and a few don't require any sewing at all. Take a look at the Basic Sewing Kit to the right, and then look at the What You Need list for each project before you start.

Basic Techniques

It's hard to find an easier fabric to work with than felt, so most of the techniques used in this book are quite standard. As with materials, feel free to go your own way: The embroidery police won't knock on our door if the instructions say to whipstitch, but you decide a blanket stitch would look better.

USING TEMPLATES

All of the templates for the projects in this book can be found starting on page 112. For medium to large pattern pieces, enlarge the template to the appropriate percentage and cut it out. Then pin the template onto the felt, and cut out the shape. For especially small or intricate shapes, cut out the paper template,

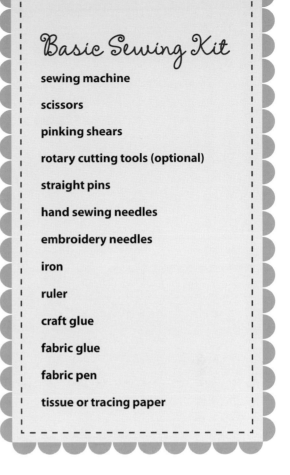

Basic Sewing Kit

- **sewing machine**
- **scissors**
- **pinking shears**
- **rotary cutting tools (optional)**
- **straight pins**
- **hand sewing needles**
- **embroidery needles**
- **iron**
- **ruler**
- **craft glue**
- **fabric glue**
- **fabric pen**
- **tissue or tracing paper**

pin it to the felt, and then use a disappearing fabric marker to trace around the template, directly onto the felt. (Test your fabric markers on a piece of scrap felt first—some disappear better than others.) Use the traced lines to cut.

For patterns with embroidery designs, enlarge the embroidery design to the appropriate percentage, and then transfer the design to your felt. If you're using a light felt color, you may be able to place the felt on top of the pattern and trace the stitch lines with a disappearing fabric marker. For intricate embroidery patterns that may take a while to complete, use a water-soluble fabric marker instead of a disappearing one. An alternative method (that works well on felt too dark to see through) is to trace the embroidery pattern onto tissue paper, and pin the tissue paper in place on the felt piece to be embroidered. Embroider the designs (through both the felt and the paper). Tear away the tissue paper. You may need to use a needle or tweezers to pull out pieces from underneath your stitches.

FINISHING FELT

Have we made it clear enough that we love the fact that felt doesn't fray? This is one of the characteristics of the material that makes it so wonderful for holiday decorations. The edges of your projects can be finished (or not) in all kinds of different ways:

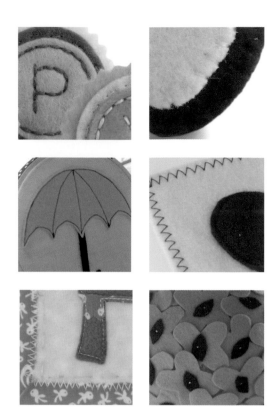

- There's something just plain sweet about pinked edges, as in the colorful Cake Toppers (page 103).

- The blanket stitch gives a look that says "made by hand and proud of it." See the Apple for Teacher Brooch (page 50).

- Machine stitch around the outside edge of your felt pieces for a polished look, as in April Showers (page 46).

- For a machine-stitched edge with pizzazz, try the zigzag stitch, as in Blooming Valentines (page 28).

- For an "unfinished finish" that's unmistakably handmade, use straight or running stitches as in the Piñata Ornaments (page 52).

- Or skip the stitching altogether: See the Mistletoe Kissing Ball (page 92).

FREE-MOTION STITCHING

Free-motion stitching takes practice, practice, and then, poof!, it's easy. If you're new to this technique, try it out on some scrap fabric first. To begin, drop or cover your machine's feed dogs (those little grabbers that come up through the metal plate to feed your fabric through the machine). Then attach a darning or free-motion foot. (You can also sew without a foot, but do so at your own risk—watch your fingers!) With free-motion sewing, the threaded needle acts as a pencil and your fabric as the paper, but you don't make your design by moving the needle; instead you move the fabric. To do so, place your fabric under the darning or free-motion foot and make a few stitches to secure the thread. Then place one hand on each side of the fabric and move the fabric to create your design as you sew. (Some sewers use rubber gloves or special quilting gloves to keep a better grip on the fabric.) In the beginning, going slow and steady will help you control your design and stitches. Eventually, you'll be able to go faster, and before you know it, you'll be feeling free and having so much fun, it'll be hard to stop.

Safety Note: Always supervise children when they are playing with handmade projects, and be sure items within their reach are age appropriate. Some of the projects in this book contain small parts that may present a choking hazard.

Embroidery Stitches

Embroidery and felt just seem made for each other. Use these illustrations to help you with any unfamiliar stitches.

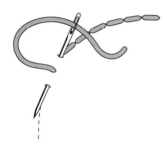

BACKSTITCH

This simple stitch creates a solid line, so it's great for outlining shapes or creating text.

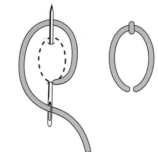

LAZY DAISY

Make a small loop and then anchor it with a single stitch at the top for a decorative stitch that resembles a flower petal.

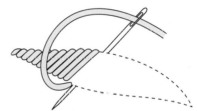

SATIN STITCH

The satin stitch is composed of parallel rows of straight stitches and is often used to fill in an outline.

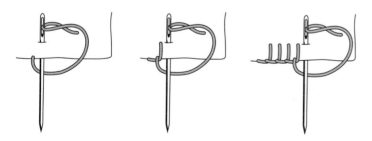

BLANKET STITCH

The blanket stitch is both decorative and functional. Use this stitch to accentuate an edge or to attach an appliqué.

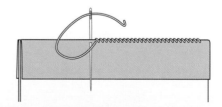

WHIPSTITCH

Also called the overcast stitch, the whipstitch is used to bind edges to prevent raveling or for decorative purposes. Simply stitch over the edge of the fabric.

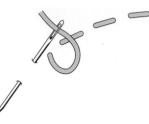

RUNNING STITCH

Make this stitch by weaving the needle through the fabric at evenly spaced intervals.

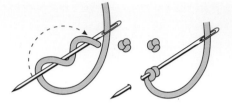

FRENCH KNOT

This elegant little knot adds interest and texture when embroidering or embellishing.

SINGLE-THREADED RUNNING STITCH

This stitch starts with a basic line of running stitches. Then, working on the top of the felt, weave a single length of floss under the stitches to create a wave-like stitch.

STEM STITCH

This is also known as a crewel stitch and is often used to outline a shape. Working from left to right, keep the floss to the right of the needle so that it always emerges from the left side of the previous stitch.

DOUBLE-THREADED RUNNING STITCH

This stitch is very similar to the single-threaded running stitch, but it uses two strands of woven floss instead of one.

SPLIT STITCH

This stitch is similar to the stem stitch, but as you bring the needle backward along the line, you poke it back through the previous stitch, splitting the strands of floss.

Projects

Are you ready for page

after page of projects that will inspire you

to create super cute

decorations and gifts for each season and

special occasion?  Good! Gather

your felt, thread your needle,

and don't forget to have fun.

Happy heart-felt celebrations!

This banner will get your year off to a cheerful start, and it's so versatile you'll want to pull it out for every celebration!

Cheers! Banner

DESIGNER: AIMEE RAY

WHAT YOU NEED

Templates (page 119)

Basic sewing kit (page 9)

Felt in several bright colors

**60 inches (1.5 m) of red ribbon,
½ inch (1.3 cm) wide**

Red thread

**Embroidery floss in various colors to
match and contrast with the felt**

WHAT YOU DO

1 Using the templates, cut nine half circles and the letters to spell Cheers! from the various colors of felt.

2 Measure about 15 inches (38.1 cm) from one end of the ribbon, and use that as your starting point to overlap the ribbon over the half circles of felt by about ½ inch (1.3 cm). Pin the half circles end-to-end along the ribbon so you're left with about 15 inches (38.1 cm) of ribbon on either end. Use the running stitch and the red thread to hand stitch the ribbon to the felt, or you can machine stitch it instead.

3 Use the running stitch or any stitch of your choice to stitch the letters in place on the half circles, reserving the first and last half circles for the fireworks and star decorations.

4 Trace the fireworks and star embroidery patterns onto tissue paper and pin them securely in place onto the remaining felt pieces. Use the running stitch and French knots (page 12) to embroider the designs (through both the paper and felt).

5 Tear away the tissue paper. You may need to use a needle or tweezers to pull out little pieces from underneath your stitches. Done! Open a bottle of something bubbly to celebrate.

No time to sew during the holiday season? Fusible web makes this a simple project to celebrate the start of a new year.

No-Sew Wine Bags

DESIGNER: STEPHANIE LYNN LIEBERT

WHAT YOU NEED

Templates (page 125)

Basic sewing kit (page 9)

2 pieces of cream felt, each about 8 x 48 inches (20.3 x 121.9 cm), plus scraps

Wine or champagne bottle

¼- to ½-inch wide (6 mm to 1.3 cm) fusible web strips (optional, you can sew instead)

Foam ball, 3 Inches (7.6 cm) in diameter

Serrated knife

Scraps of unbleached woven cotton

Wooden skewer

Hot glue gun and glue stick

White organdy ribbon, 24 to 28 inches (61 to 71.1 cm)

Hammer and nail or drill and drill bit

Clean metal jar lid, 2½ inches (6.4 cm) in diameter

Silver glitter

WHAT YOU DO

1 Fold one piece of the felt to form an 8 x 24-inch (20.3 x 61 cm) rectangle, and arrange it on your work surface so the 8-inch (20.3 cm) crease is at the bottom. Trim 1 inch (2.5 cm) off each 24-inch (61 cm) side of the felt with pinking shears, leaving the felt 6 inches (15.2 cm) wide. (Since wine and champagne bottles vary in size, you may need to adjust these measurements.)

2 Lay the bottle flat down on the felt, with its bottom at the fold, and measure 1 inch (2.5 cm) up from the top of the bottle— lightly mark a guideline.

3 To outline the hole for the wine bag, sit the bottle upright, positioned in the center of the felt strip, with the top edge of the bottle resting on the guideline. Trace around the bottom of the bottle with a fabric marker.

4 To cut the circle out of the top layer of the felt only, pinch the top layer and cut a small slit into the center of the circle you just drew. Slide your pinking shears in the slit and cut out the circle.

5 Seam the sides with the fusible web, or use machine stitching or hand stitching, leaving a 1-inch (2.5 cm) opening at the bottom crease. For fusible web, cut two strips, one for each side. Place each strip in between the felt as close to the outer edges of each side as possible (remembering to leave a 1-inch [2.5 cm] opening at the bottom on each side). Lightly press with a steam iron set to the wool setting for about 30 seconds to fuse. Keep the iron moving at all times when placed on the felt—it can melt the felt if left in one spot.

6 Once the sides are together, align the top edges and trim with the pinking shears (the amount you need to cut will depend on the size of your wine bottle), and then seam the top in the same fashion. Since the felt has a little give, the bottle should slide perfectly into the opening in the bag. Repeat all steps to make a second wine bag.

(to make the rag flower ornament)

1 Begin by cutting the polystyrene ball in half with a serrated knife.

2 Cut several 1-inch-wide (2.5 cm) strips of the unbleached woven cotton, and then cut the strips into 1-inch (2.5 cm) squares. (They don't have to be perfectly square.)

3 Place the half ball flat side down on a protected work surface. Working in small sections, squirt some craft glue onto the foam ball; then using the sharp end of a wooden skewer, poke the center of a fabric square into the polystyrene. Continue doing this until the entire surface is covered, placing the squares fairly close to one another.

4 Hot glue 12 to 14 inches (30.5 x 35.6 cm) of the organdy ribbon to the back for a hanger.

(to make the felt flower ornament)

1 Use the hammer and nail or the drill and drill bit to make a hole near the edge of the jar lid. You'll use this to thread the ribbon onto the ornament.

2 Copy and cut out the large petal template, and use it to cut 11 or 12 petals from the felt.

3 Hot glue the petals around the outer edge of the lid.

4 Use the small petal template to cut about 15 petals. Hot glue these petals to the lid, working from the outer edge in, and overlapping the first layer of petals. When you get to the center, you'll have to trim the last two petals to fit, folding and tucking them in.

5 Place a dab of hot glue in the center and sprinkle the silver glitter on top. Dust off any excess glitter once the glue has dried. Finish by threading 12 to 14 inches (30.5 to 35.6 cm) of the organdy ribbon through the drilled hole for a hanger.

This garland commemorates
Martin Luther King Day, but it
would also look nice in a child's
room or classroom all year long.

I Have a Dream Garland

DESIGNER: KATHY SHELDON

WHAT YOU NEED

Template (page 119)

Basic sewing kit (page 9)

Brown, tan, and cream felt (or your choice of colors)

Tan or invisible thread

WHAT YOU DO

1 Use the template to cut both girls and boys from the various colors of felt. You can cut out all girls and then just trim off the ponytail and cut the felt to turn the dress into shorts if that's easier.

2 Using the photo for reference, lay the felt figures out across a table or other large flat surface in the order you want them in your garland, paying attention to the order of colors and boy or girl, and the direction each is facing (most felt looks pretty much the same on both sides, so feel free to flip them over).

3 Starting at the far left, gather the children one at a time and pile one on top of the other, until you have a stack with the last child on the right at the top of the stack.

4 Before you begin to sew, pull the thread coming from the bobbin and needle so that it's longer than usual—you'll use this to hang one side of the garland. Starting from the top of your stack, stitch across the arms and chest of each child, feeding the figures through the sewing machine one after another without breaking the threads after stitching each one.

5 When you have stitched all the figures together, pull another long length of the threads for hanging, and cut. Knot the threads at both ends near the first and last figure, and your garland is ready for you to hang.

Welcome the Chinese
New Year with this
adorable lantern
embroidered with
koi and the Chinese
symbol for luck.

Chinese Luck Lantern

DESIGNER: AIMEE RAY

WHAT YOU NEED

Templates (page 128)

Basic sewing kit (page 9)

Red and yellow felt,
9 x 12 inches (22.9 x 30.5 cm) each

Yellow and red thread

Polyfill stuffing

Yellow, light pink,
and black embroidery floss

Tissue paper

WHAT YOU DO

1 Using the templates, cut out all the red and yellow felt pieces.

2 Use the yellow thread to stitch one of the yellow side-end pieces over one pointy end of one of the red pieces. Repeat until each end of all the five red pieces has been covered with a yellow side-end piece.

3 Stitch the top cap and the top cap edge together, using the whipstitch and yellow thread, trapping an end of the handle in the seam at either side. Stitch the two ends of the top cap edge together. Tuck a bit of the polyfill stuffing inside the cap. Cut the fringe as shown on the template, and then use the yellow thread to stitch the two edges of the fringe piece together to form a cylinder.

4 Embroider the designs onto the red side pieces, using the colors shown in the photograph or any colors of your choice. Trace the embroidery patterns onto tissue paper and pin them securely in place onto the felt pieces. Embroider the designs (through both the felt and the paper). Tear away the tissue paper. You may need to use a needle or tweezers to pull out pieces from underneath your stitches.

5 Now line up two of the side pieces and stitch them together along one edge, using yellow and red thread. Repeat, alternating blank and embroidered pieces, until all but the last two edges are stitched together. Stuff the ball firmly with polyfill, and then stitch up the last two edges.

6 Use yellow thread to stitch the top cap and the bottom fringe onto the ball.

This sweet little groundhog will keep your phone or handheld device safe and secure, and its shadow will let you know when spring is coming!

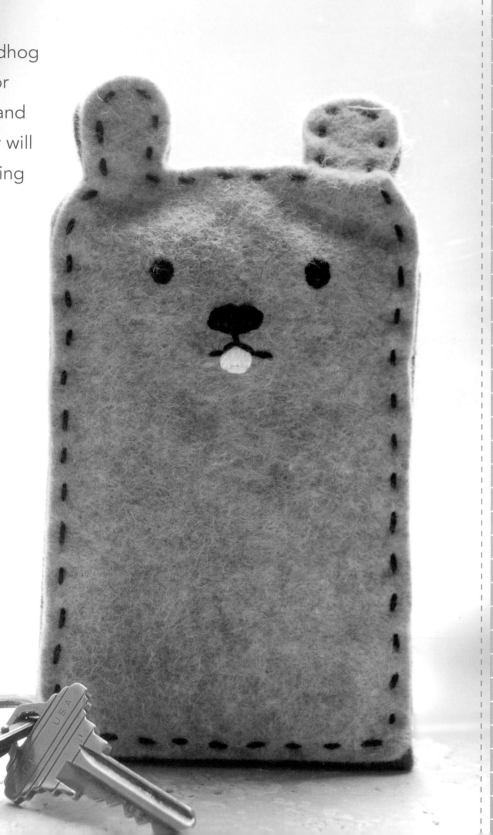

Seeing Shadows Phone Case

DESIGNER: MOLLIE JOHANSON

WHAT YOU NEED

Templates (page 117)

Basic sewing kit (page 9)

Light brown and dark gray felt

Black and white embroidery floss

2 sew-on snaps, size 1

WHAT YOU DO

1 Using the templates, cut out two groundhog bodies from the light brown felt and one shadow from the dark gray felt.

2 Transfer the face pattern to one of the groundhog bodies. Using six strands of embroidery floss and the backstitch and the satin stitch, stitch the eyes, nose, and mouth with the black floss, and stitch the tooth with the white floss. This is the front.

3 Sew one side of the snaps to the ears of the shadow. Sew the other side of the snaps to the ears of the plain groundhog body—this is the back.

4 Place the shadow on a flat surface so the side with snaps is facing down. Place the front body piece right side up, positioned so its bottom only overlaps the shadow's bottom by about ¾ inch (1.9 cm). Pin the pieces together. (The ears of the shadow should match up with the ears of the body when folded up.) Sew the overlapping pieces together along the bottom edge of the front piece using the running stitch and six strands of black embroidery floss, and stop, but don't tie off your floss, once you've stitched across the entire bottom.

5 Pin the front and back body pieces together, making sure to leave the shadow free. Starting at the bottom near the shadow, continue to sew around the front and back of the groundhog only, with the running stitch and the black floss. Stop when you get to the other side of the shadow. Tie off at the back.

6 Slide your handheld device inside, then fold the shadow up behind the groundhog and secure the snaps.

Stacked hearts embellished with a pair
of tiny toadstools—a perfect Valentine's
woodland whimsy.

Mushroom Love Brooch

DESIGNER: LISA JORDAN

WHAT YOU NEED

Templates (page 125)

Basic sewing kit (page 9)

Turquoise, white, yellow, and red felted garment wool or wool felt

Dark gray felt (optional, see Tip)

White, red, turquoise, and yellow embroidery floss

Pin back

Fabric glue (optional)

WHAT YOU DO

1 Using the templates, cut one small heart from the turquoise felt, one medium heart from the white felt, and one large heart from the yellow felt. Cut an additional large heart from the dark gray felt, and set aside. Use the templates to cut the two small half-circles from the red felt for the mushroom caps and the V shape from the white felt for the mushroom stems.

Tip: To simplify, cut the second large heart shape, which will be the brooch back, from the yellow felt instead of dark gray.

2 Using the photo for reference, position the mushroom stems on the turquoise heart, and whipstitch them in place with a single strand of the white floss. Add a few small running stitches down the center of the V to help define the two stems. Use one strand of the red floss to whipstitch a red mushroom cap on top of each stem.

3 Thread your needle with two strands of white embroidery floss and add a few decorative French knots (page 12) to the mushroom caps.

4 Stack the turquoise heart on top of the white heart, and stitch them together using the whipstitch and three strands of the turquoise floss. Then stitch this stack of hearts onto the large yellow heart, using three strands of red floss and the running stitch. Set aside.

5 Sew a pin back to the felt backing piece. (If you like, you can cover the base of the pin back with a small felt heart.) Then position the heart stack on the backing, tacking it in place with the fabric glue if desired. Begin sewing the stack to the backing using a blanket stitch and three strands of the yellow embroidery floss. Stitch around the entire piece, hiding the knot beneath the stitches.

Take some blank cards,
a few sheets of felt,
and some leftover felt
scraps, and you'll have
a rainbow of valentines
to share with those
you love.

Blooming Valentines

DESIGNER: REBEKAH J. CHAMBERLIN

WHAT YOU NEED

Templates (page 127)

Basic sewing kit (page 9)

Blank white greeting cards

Assortment of felt sheets and scraps (see Tip)

Thread in matching and contrasting colors

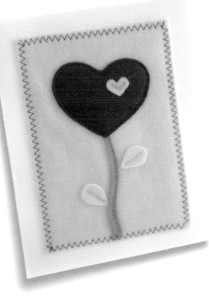

WHAT YOU DO

(to make the card)

1   Measure your card and cut your background felt rectangle accordingly, allowing room for the white front of the card to show around the felt. With the card folded, cut the right side edges with pinking shears if desired.

Tip: The kind of felt that's available as stiffened sheets can be used for the background piece.

2   Lightly tack the felt background in place with a few dabs of craft or fabric glue and allow to dry. Using the zigzag stitch and a contrasting color of thread, stitch around the edge of the felt.

3   Use the templates to cut the shapes for the heart flowers, adjusting sizes if needed for the size of your blank card.

4   Arrange all of the cutout flower pieces onto the felt rectangle and lightly tack them in place with craft or fabric glue. Next change your thread color and stitch the stem and leaves in place with one

stitch right down the middle of each piece. Last of all, stitch carefully around the perimeter of your heart bloom and use a couple of stitches to secure the tiny heart in place.

(to make the envelope)

1   Add ½ inch (1.3 cm) to your card's dimensions, and cut two pieces of felt to that size for an envelope. Also cut one 1¼ x 1½-inch (3.2 x 3.8 cm) piece of felt, and pink the edges to create a stamp.

2   Snip out a small heart from red felt. Stitch the heart onto the stamp with red thread, then stitch the stamp onto the envelope with red thread.

3   Place the two pieces of felt wrong sides together and sew around three sides with contrasting thread, leaving one end open to slide the card in. Pink the edges of your envelope if desired.

You'll be tempted to leave these baubles up all year—and they're so easy to sew, you can make them in multiples!

Heart Baubles

DESIGNER: LAURA HOWARD

WHAT YOU NEED

(to make one bauble)

Templates (page 125)

Basic sewing kit (page 9)

Red felt, 6½ x 5 inches (16.5 x 12.7 cm)

Light turquoise felt, 2½ x 2½ inches (6.4 x 6.4 cm)

White felt, 2¾ x 2¾ inches (7 x 7 cm)

Red and light turquoise thread

Narrow red gingham ribbon, 5 inches (12.7 cm)

WHAT YOU DO

1 Using the templates, cut one heart shape from the red felt, one small circle from the turquoise felt, one medium circle from the white felt, and two large circles from the red felt.

2 Using the photo for reference, arrange one of each size circle in a pile, with the heart in the center of the top circle. (Put the second red circle aside for now.) Hold all four layers together and sew around the edge of the heart, using the running stitch and the red thread, making sure to sew through all the layers.

3 Use the running stitch and the turquoise matching thread to stitch around the edge of the turquoise circle.

4 Fold the ribbon over to form a loop, then sew the ends in place at the top of the plain red circle using the whipstitch and the red thread. The ribbon ends should overlap the felt by about ½ inch (1.3 cm).

5 Align and pin the remaining red circle to the back of the bauble, with the ribbon loop at the top and the ribbon ends sandwiched between the layers. Use the running stitch and red thread to stitch around the edge of the bauble, sewing flush with the edge of the white circle. Finish your stitching neatly at the back.

This wee leprechaun comes with his own pot of gold and rainbow—whipstitch him up and you're sure to have good luck.

Leprechaun Finger Puppet

DESIGNER: CATHY GAUBERT

WHAT YOU NEED

Templates (page 118)

Basic sewing kit (page 9)

Light green wool felt, 4 x 4 inches (10.2 x 10.2 cm) (body and hat band)

Dark green wool felt, 2 x 2 inches (5.1 x 5.1 cm)

Tan wool felt, 3 x 3 inches (7.6 x 7.6 cm)

Rust wool felt, 3 x 3 inches (7.6 x 7.6 cm)

Black wool felt, 3 x 4 inches (7.6 x 10.2 cm)

Yellow wool felt, 1 x 2 inches (2.5 x 5.1 cm)

White wool felt, 3 x 4 inches (7.6 x 10.2 cm)

Red, orange, yellow, green, blue, indigo, and violet wool felt strips, each 1½ x 4 inches (3.8 x 10.2 cm)

Dark green, light green, rust, brown, red, and black embroidery floss (or thread)

Clear thread

WHAT YOU DO

(to make the leprechaun)

1 Use the templates to cut two body pieces and one hat band from the light green felt, two arms from the dark green felt, one head piece from the tan felt, one beard and one head piece from the auburn felt (this is for the back of the head), and two hat pieces from the black felt.

2 Use two strands of floss for all stitching. Using the dark green floss and the photo for placement, whipstitch the arms onto one of the body pieces.

3 Use the light green floss and the satin stitch to embroider a four-leaf clover onto the body, right above the hands.

4 With brown floss and the backstitch, embroider the eyes and eyebrows onto the face. Use the red floss to backstitch the mouth.

5 Place the beard onto the face and use the rust floss and the whipstitch to attach the upper part of the beard.

6 Using the photo for reference, place the embroidered face piece so it just overlaps the top of the body. Whipstitch through the bottom edge of the beard and face with the rust floss to attach the head to the top of the body.

7 Turn the body over and place the rust back of the head onto the backside of the face, making sure the head front and back match up. Whipstitch the front and back of the head together, starting at one side of the neck, going around the top of the head, and continuing on to the other side of the neck.

8 Match body pieces, sliding the top of the back body under the backside of the head, and pin. Whipstitch the bottom of the head to the top back of the body with rust floss. (Slide your finger into the leprechaun's head to hold the felt together as you stitch this part.) Use light green floss to whipstitch the body sides together, leaving the bottom open.

9 Attach the light green band to the front of one hat piece by embroidering a buckle with the yellow floss (four simple stitches: two vertical going across the band, one horizontal going above the band, and one horizontal going below the band). Use the black floss and the whipstitch to begin stitching the hat to-gether, starting at point A and stitching over the hat's top to point B, leaving the bottom open.

10 Place the hat onto the leprechaun's head at a jaunty angle, and continue stitching through both layers of hat and head until you are back to point A.

(to make the pot of gold and rainbow)

1 Use the templates to cut two cloud pieces from the white felt, one gold piece from the yellow felt, and two pot pieces from the black felt.

2 Stack the rainbow strips in ROYGBIV order. Use clear thread to hand stitch through all layers. (About six running stitches roughly ½ inch (1.3 cm) long, straight down the middle should do it.)

3 Place the cloud pieces together. Whipstitch from A to B with the white floss. Insert one end of the rainbow (red side up) between B and C, and then whip-stitch the top of the cloud to point C, securing the top of the red strip inside the cloud with your stitches as you do so. Continue stitching the cloud pieces together from C to D. Then turn the cloud over and stitch the back (from C to B), this time securing the top of the violet strip inside as you do so.

4 Use six strands of yellow floss and French knots (see page 12) to attach the gold piece to the front of one pot piece. Use the black floss to whipstitch the pot together in the same manner as you did the cloud, inserting the rainbow inside the layers of the pot and leaving the bottom of the pot open so a finger or two can fit inside.

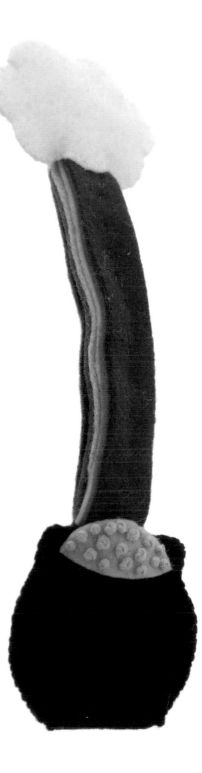

Here's an adorable bunting
you can hang Easter after Easter,
and it will never get stale!

Bunny Bunting

DESIGNER: DANA WILLARD

WHAT YOU NEED

Template (page 117)

Basic Sewing Kit (page 9)

Pink or yellow felt, about ½ yard (.5 m) or less

Pencil (or other small round object)

Brown fabric paint

White muslin (or other fabric, ribbon, or colored twine)

Serger (optional)

Pink or yellow thread

Turquoise thread (optional)

Eyelet (optional)

Add an eyelet and ribbon to a single bunny for a cute door hanger.

WHAT YOU DO

1 Fold your felt in half (because each bunny is a double layer), and use the template to cut out as many bunnies as you'd like.

Tip: You can make single-layered bunnies to save time and felt, but they tend to look less polished and a bit see-through.

2 Line your bunny fronts up on a piece of scrap paper. Dip a pencil eraser or another small round object into the brown fabric paint and dab it onto each bunny to make the eyes and nose. (With the beloved marshmallow confections, each face in a box is slightly different—not to mention a bit squished sometimes! So don't worry about being precise or even symmetrical.)

3 Let your bunnies dry for at least an hour. If you're antsy, you can speed up the process with a blow dryer, but be careful that they don't fly all over the place!

4 While you're waiting for the faces to dry, prep the material you'll use to hang the bunnies. My favorite method is to cut strips of a double layer of muslin, sew the strips together to make one very long strip, and serge the edges with pink or turquoise thread. You can use any fabric in this same way or just use ribbon or colored twine.

5 The quick and easy way to attach your bunnies to your bunting is to align one bunny back with a bunny front and sew the double-layered bunny to your ribbon by the ears—then just keep going in this fashion until you're bunnied out.

6 A slightly longer method (which will result in a stronger, more polished-looking bunting) is to sew each bunny back to the ribbon while the faces are drying: Lay one down on your ribbon, sew across the ears, grab the next bunny back and repeat. Once you've attached all the bunny backs, align the decorated bunnies on top, and sew an outline all the way around each one.

This little guy wants
to hop right up
on your table and
sit awhile.

Bunny Pal

DESIGNER: CATHY GAUBERT

WHAT YOU NEED

Templates (page 116)

Basic sewing kit (page 9)

Brown felt, 12 x 12 inches
(30.5 x 30.5 cm)

Scraps of pink, black, yellow,
lavender, and aqua felt

White felt, 3 x 6 inches (7.6 x 15.2 cm)

Pink, black, yellow, lavender,
and aqua embroidery floss

Brown thread

Stuffing

Black embroidery floss

Embroidery floss to match
the egg's dots

Extra long needle

Heavy brown thread

Cream-colored heavy thread
or carpet thread (for whiskers)

Wool yarn (for tail)

Pompom maker (optional)

White thread

WHAT YOU DO

(to make the bunny)

1   Use the template to cut out six head pieces, and two each of the body, ear, arm, and leg pieces. Place two head pieces together, and begin stitching at the top point all the way to the bottom (the neck), leaving the bottom open. Add the next piece, again matching the top points and then stitching top to bottom. Put this section aside.

2   Stitch the remaining three pieces together in the same manner. You'll now have two sections (the front and the back of the head).

3   Place one ear piece on top of a piece of brown felt, and stitch about 1/8 inch (3 mm) in from the edge. Repeat with the second ear. Cut out both double ear shapes.

4   With right sides facing, pin the ears to the front of the head (about 1/2 inch [1.3 cm] in from either side of the point where all three head pieces meet at the top), basting in place.

5   With right sides still facing, match that same top point on both head sections (making sure the ears are tucked inside the head and out of needle's reach), and then stitch, beginning at the top point, down one side to the neck opening.

Turn the head and stitch the other side in the same manner. (You'll be going through quite a few layers, so go slowly and carefully.) Gently turn the head right side out.

6   Now for the face! Cut out two pink and two black felt circles for the eyes. Place one black circle onto one pink for each eye. Referring to the photos for placement, pin each eye to the bunny's head. Using six strands of the black floss, attach each eye by going in through the head opening, coming up through the pupil of one of the eyes and then back down through that pupil to attach the eye to the head.

7   The nose is essentially a stitched Y with a long stem. Mark the four points of the Y on the felt with pins for placement. Using six strands of the pink floss, go in through the neck opening and come out at the top right side of the Y. Run the floss under the center pin, and then go back in through the top left side of the Y. Come up through the very bottom point on the Y, and loop the floss around the strands that are under the pin in the center. Pull the floss taut, and go back in at the same point at the bottom of the Y. Tie off inside the head and then stuff the head firmly.

8   Next, make the arms and legs in the same manner as the ears. Be sure to lay the limbs onto the felt facing opposite directions or you'll end up with two left feet (and arms!). Refer to the marks on the template, and place the arms on the body and baste in place.

9   Pin the body pieces right sides together. Using a ¼-inch (6 mm) seam allowance, begin at point A and stitch around the body, ending at point B (leave the bottom open). Turn right side out, partially stuff the body, and set aside.

10   Cut two 3 x ¾-inch (7.6 x 1.9 cm) strips from the brown felt for the bunny's bottom. Baste the legs to one of the strips about ½ inch (1.3 cm) in from either side, making sure the feet are facing each other (figure 1). Place the second felt strip on top with the legs sandwiched in between. Using ¼-inch (6 mm) seam allowance, stitch straight across the top long side of the rectangles, catching the top of the legs in the seam (figure 2). Lift the top layer of felt and you'll have a 3 x 1½-inch (7.6 x 3.8 cm) bunny bottom with legs (figure 3).

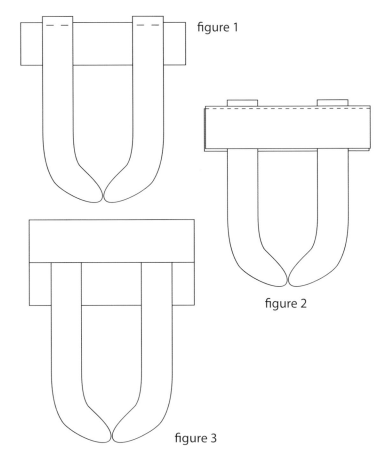

figure 1

figure 2

figure 3

11 Find the middle of the bunny's front and the middle of the bottom piece you sewed in the last step, line up, and pin together. Match the side seams on the body with the middle seam of the bottom piece, pin the bottom to the body, and begin hand stitching to attach the bottom and its legs to the body. When you have about 1½ to 2 inches (3.8 to 5.1 cm) left to stitch, add more stuffing until the body is very firmly packed. Finish stitching to close the bottom. Set aside.

12 Use a 30-inch (76.2 cm) length of the heavy brown thread and the running stitch to slightly close the bottom of the head. Be sure to leave a space for the neck to fit—if your thumb fits in, that should be the right amount of space. It's important that you don't snip the thread yet! You'll use the remaining length to attach the head to the body.

13 Thread the extra long needle using the thread still attached to the head. Place the head onto the neck and stitch back and forth through the head and neck to attach the head securely to the body. If it seems wobbly, go back around one more time with your stitching. Knot the thread and pull it through the body to sink the knot. Snip the thread.

14 Honestly, the easiest way to make a pompom for the tail is to buy a pompom maker from a craft store and follow the manufacturer's directions. These simple gadgets cost little and will change your life when it comes to pompom-hood. To make one the old fashioned way, wrap about 20 yards (18.3 m) of wool yarn around the four fingers of one hand lots and lots of times. Gently ease the yarn off your fingers, and wrap a 20-inch (50.8 cm) length of thread around the middle of the loops, pulling tightly to gather up the yarn, before tying it off. Snip the loops on either side. Fluff up the yarn and trim any stray pieces. Hand stitch it to the bunny's backside using the attached thread.

15 To add whiskers to each side of the bunny's head, thread your needle with a double strand of the cream-colored heavy thread or carpet thread, make a tiny stitch on one side of the face, and then knot the four strands of thread tight against the head. Trim the whiskers to match. Repeat on the other side of the head.

(to make the egg)

1 Cut two egg pieces out of white felt. Stitch these right sides together with the white thread, leaving an opening for turning and stuffing. Turn right side out, stuff firmly, and stitch closed. Cut out small and medium circles from the yellow, lavender, and aqua felt scraps (you can use the two eye templates for these circles). Attach these to the egg with matching floss, using a simple X stitch, and hiding the knots under the circles.

2 Join the bunny's arms together to hold the egg by overlapping the ends of the arms and taking one or two stitches to secure. Now you can slip the egg into the bunny's arms. Ah, happy bunny!

Easter egg trees are a tradition in Eastern Europe. Mix and match the elements of these eggs for different combinations.

Easter Egg Tree Ornaments

DESIGNER: KATHY SHELDON

WHAT YOU NEED

(to make the bunny)

Templates (page 115)

Basic sewing kit (page 9)

Orange, light blue, cream, and gold felt

Cream, brown, gold, sage green, light blue, and orange embroidery floss

Embroidery scissors

Stuffing

Decorative ribbon

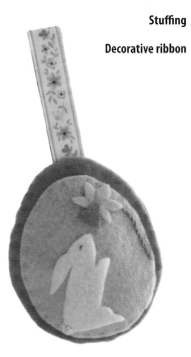

WHAT YOU DO

1 Use the templates to cut two large egg shapes from the orange felt, one small egg shape from the light blue felt, the bunny from the cream felt, the daffodil's "cup" from the orange felt, and the daffodil petals from the gold felt.

2 Using the photo as a guide, position the bunny onto the light blue egg and adhere with the fabric glue. Using three strands of cream embroidery floss, add five French knots (page 12) to give the bunny's tail some fluff. Use one strand of brown embroidery floss to stitch the bunny's eye.

3 Use embroidery scissors to cut tiny triangles from the wide end of the daffodil cup to frill it.

Tip: Curved manicure scissors are also great for cutting small details in felt—keep a dedicated set in your sewing kit. To turn light blue circles of felt into the forget-me-not blooms on the other eggs, simply snip five evenly spaced curved Vs into each circle and then add a yellow French knot to each center.

4 Using the photo as a guide, attach the gold daffodil petals to the blue egg with fabric glue. Then glue the orange daffodil cup on top of the petal, positioned as shown in the photo. Use two strands of gold embroidery floss to add decorative stitches to define the petal shapes and the top of the cup.

5 Using four strands of sage green embroidery floss, use the stem stitch (page 12) to add a stem to the daffodil.

6 Use two strands of the light blue embroidery floss and the running stitch (or any stitch of your choice) to attach the light blue egg to one large orange egg.

7 Align and pin the plain orange egg to the to the back of the embellished orange egg, with the ribbon loop at the top and the ends sandwiched between the layers. Use the running stitch and orange floss to sew around the edge of the eggs (or use the blanket stitch for a slightly different look). When you've stitched most of the way, stuff the egg to the desired state of plumpness. Continue stitching around the entire egg and hide the knot.

Show your love
for our small blue
planet with these
earth-toned leaf
garlands.

Earth Day Leaf Garlands

DESIGNER: AIMEE RAY

WHAT YOU NEED

Templates (page 121)

Basic sewing kit (page 9)

Felt in several colors of green, blue, and brown

18 inches (45.7 cm) of satin or grosgrain ribbon, ½ inch (1.3 cm) wide

Embroidery floss in greens, blues, and browns

WHAT YOU DO

1 Use the templates to cut out five small leaf shapes and five large leaf shapes for each ribbon.

2 Cut notches into some of the large and small leaves, aiming for an even number of plain and notched leaves in both sets.

3 Starting at the bottom of the ribbon, place a large notched leaf on the ribbon, and then a small plain leaf on top. Use the embroidery floss in different colors to stitch various designs through all three layers to secure the leaves in place. For some leaves, add a running stitch down the middle with single stitches to each side to create veins. For others, scatter straight stitches along either side of the leaf center. Let the photos inspire your color combinations and stitch patterns.

4 Continue adding leaves to the ribbon, an inch or two apart, varying colors, as well as whether the large or small leaf part is notched.

Though April showers may come your way, these umbrella hangings will brighten even the rainiest of days.

April Showers

DESIGNER: AMANDA CARESTIO

WHAT YOU NEED

(to make the blue umbrella)

Templates (page 112)

Basic sewing kit (page 9)

Blue felt, 5 x 5 inches (12.7 x 12.7 cm)

Black felt, 1 x 5 inches (2.5 x 12.7 cm)

Felt for backing, 7 x 7 inches (17.8 x 17.8 cm)

Linen, 8 x 8 inches (20.3 x 20.3 cm)

5-inch (12.7 cm) embroidery hoop

Black and white thread

3/8-inch-wide (9.5 mm) polka dot ribbon, 16 inches (40.6 cm)

WHAT YOU DO

1 Use the templates to cut the umbrella shape out of the blue felt and the handle from the black felt.

2 Position the handle and umbrella in place on the linen, making sure they'll fit inside the embroidery hoop, and adhere with fabric glue. Let dry completely.

3 Machine stitch the umbrella shape in place with the black thread. Hand stitch over the base of the handle with the white thread.

4 Center the umbrella in the hoop. Cut off the excess linen from the edge.

5 Apply glue to the back of the hoop, and then set the hoop on top of the backing felt. Let dry, then cut around the edge of the hoop, removing the excess felt. Glue the polka dot ribbon to the edge of the hoop.

Look what those April showers brought—a May flowers garland that's perfect for celebrating May Day!

May Flowers Garland

DESIGNER: AMANDA CARESTIO

WHAT YOU NEED

Template (page 123)

Basic sewing kit (page 9)

Fusible web

Green and white fabric scraps or fabric of your choice (or a fat quarter)

Cream felt scraps

Craft knife

Light green yarn

Yarn needle

WHAT YOU DO

1 Trace the circle template onto the back of the fusible web multiple times (you'll need two circles for each flower).

2 Iron the fusible web to the back of the fabric. Cut out the circles using the lines you drew in step one. Remove the paper backing.

3 With a pressing cloth, iron the fabric circles onto the cream felt, placing the circles close together, but not touching.

4 Cut around each circle with pinking shears, leaving a little felt showing at the edges.

5 With the craft knife, cut two slits in the center of each flower, through both the fabric and the felt.

6 Thread the yarn on the yarn needle. For double-sided flowers, stack two fabric and felt flowers, felt backs together. Place two flower shapes face down on your workspace. Working from the back of one flower shape, stitch the yarn through the left slit, back in through the right slit, through the left slit of the second flower layer, and back in the right slit.

Knot the yarn to itself (hiding the knot between the flower layers), and continue adding flowers, one about every 5 or 6 inches (12.7 or 15.2 cm).

7 Knot a loop in each end of the garland for hanging.

Want to be the teacher's pet? Show your appreciation with this sweet apple brooch.

Apple for Teacher Brooch

DESIGNER: LISA JORDAN

WHAT YOU NEED

Templates (page 112)

Basic sewing kit (page 9)

White, green, and red felted garment wool (page 8) or wool felt

Dark gray felt (optional, see Tip)

White, black, green, and red embroidery floss

Small scrap of leather or leather lace

Pin back

WHAT YOU DO

1 Using the templates, cut one small apple shape from the white felt, one leaf shape from the green felt, one large apple shape from the red felt, and one large apple shape from the dark gray felt.

TIP: To simplify, you can instead cut the second large apple shape, which will be the brooch back, from the red felt.

2 Position the white interior apple shape on top of one red apple shape and whip-stitch around the outside of the white piece with three strands of the white floss to attach. Backstitch down the center to make two apple halves with a small oval in the center, where the seeds will go.

3 Stitch two small apple seeds using the satin stitch and two strands of the black floss.

4 Snip a small stem from the scrap of leather. Tuck the stem into the crease at the top of the white apple interior, and place the leaf over it. Use three strands of the green floss to sew the leaf to the apple. Start by bringing the needle up

through the leather piece to hold the stem in place. Take a few stitches through the apple and the leaf, then just through the leaf when you are near the top curve of the apple.

5 Finish stitching the leaf vein, working the stitches back to the center down the underside of the leaf as if sewing a single-threaded running stitch (page 12). Give the floss a little tug to make the leaf curl a bit, and then hide the knot.

6 Sew the pin back onto the apple back. Place the embellished apple onto this back piece, tacking it in place with fabric glue if desired. Use the blanket stitch and three strands of the red floss to sew the backing to the apple. Continue around the apple, concealing the knot inside the stitches when finished.

Stitch up these adorable
piñata ornaments and
you'll be ready for a fiesta!

Piñata Ornaments

DESIGNER: AMANDA CARESTIO

WHAT YOU NEED

(to make two)

Template (page 122)

Basic sewing kit (page 9)

Turquoise fabric scraps

Orange patterned fabric, about 6 x 12 inches (15.2 x 30.5 cm), plus scraps

Fusible web

Purple felt, 4 x 6 inches (10.2 x 15.2 cm)

Cream felt, 9 x 12 inches (22.9 x 30.5 cm)

Pressing cloth

Striped ribbon, 16 inches (40.6 cm)

Yellow and turquoise embroidery floss

WHAT YOU DO

1 Iron fusible web to the back of the turquoise and orange-patterned fabric scraps, and cut into strips about ¼ inch (6 mm) wide—no need to be exact. Use pinking shears to cut some of the strips.

2 Referring to the photo for placement, iron the strips across the piece of purple felt in horizontal rows, using a pressing cloth.

3 Copy and cut out the template. Pin or trace the template onto the purple felt and the fabric strips, then cut out one piñata shape. Turn the template over, and cut out a second piñata shape.

4 From the cream felt, cut two 4 x 5-inch (10.2 x 12.7 cm) rectangles. From the orange patterned fabric, cut two 5 x 6-inch (12.7 x 15.2 cm) rectangles.

5 Center one cream felt piece on one fabric piece with wrong sides facing. Fold the edges of the fabric over onto the front of the felt, pin in place, and zigzag stitch along the edge of the fabric.

6 Cut an 8-inch (20.3 cm) strand of ribbon, fold it in half, and stitch it in place, centered on the back at the top of the decoration.

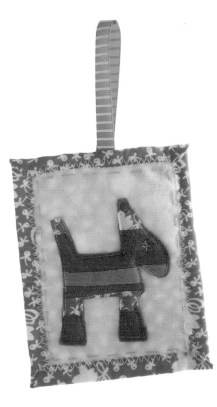

7 Use fabric glue to adhere the piñata shape in place on the center of the cream felt, and carefully stitch in place.

8 With the yellow floss, stitch an eye. With the turquoise floss, stitch a decorative running stitch around the inside edge of the cream felt.

9 Repeat steps 5 through 8 to make the second ornament.

A great gift for your mother or any tea lover, these tea bags will help keep moths from blankets and sweaters.

Lavender Tea Bag Sachets

DESIGNER: LAURA HOWARD

WHAT YOU NEED

(to make one)

Templates (page 123)

Basic sewing kit (page 9)

White felt

Scrap of pink felt

Purple felt

Tissue paper

White and purple embroidery floss

Pink, white, and purple thread

Narrow white ribbon, 5 inches (12.7 cm)

Teaspoon (or any small spoon)

Dried lavender

WHAT YOU DO

1 Use the templates provided to cut out two white tea bag shapes and one small pink heart shape. Trace the tag template (both the word "tea" and the cutting lines) onto the tissue paper and pin the paper in place onto a piece of the purple felt.

Tip: Since it's hard to embroider on a small piece of felt, it's often easier to embroider a larger piece and then cut the embroidered felt to the desired size and shape.

2 Use three strands of the white embroidery floss and a large needle to backstitch the word "tea," sewing through the paper and the felt. Don't pull your stitches too tight or the felt will pucker. Use the cutting lines on the tissue paper to cut out the tag. Tear away the tissue paper, and use a needle or tweezers to pull out any pieces left underneath your stitches.

3 Use the running stitch and the pink thread to attach the small pink heart to a piece of purple felt. Trace the cutting lines only from the tag template onto tissue paper, and center the tissue paper over the stitched pink heart. Use the cutting lines to cut out the tag shape.

4 Whipstitch one end of the narrow white ribbon to the top of one tea bag shape using the white thread, and then whipstitch the other end to the top of one tag shape using the purple thread. The ribbon ends should overlap the felt by about 3/8 inch (.95 cm).

5 Pin or hold the two purple tag shapes wrong sides together with the ribbon end sandwiched between them. Whipstitch around the edges, using the purple thread, to sew the shapes together.

6 Pin the two tea bag shapes together. Use the running stitch and three strands of purple floss to sew around the edges of the tea bags. Start where the ribbon overlaps the felt, and sew almost all the way around the tea bag, leaving a gap large enough to insert a teaspoon. Sew back along where you've just sewn, sewing between the gaps to create a continuous line of stitching.

7 Use the teaspoon to fill the tea bag sachet lightly with the dried lavender, then gently poke the handle inside to distribute the lavender evenly and into all the corners. Sew up the gap with more running stitches in purple floss, sewing along and then back as before to create a continuous line of stitching.

Show your mother how much
you love her with this heartfelt,
hand-stitched pillow!

Early Bird Pillow

DESIGNER: CATHY ZIEGELE

WHAT YOU NEED

Templates (page 115)

Basic sewing kit (page 9)

Yellow wool felt, 12 x 18 inches
(30.5 x 45.7 cm)

Hot pink, bright blue, medium pink,
light blue, and lavender wool felt,
2½ x 2½ inches (6.4 x 6.4 cm) each

Orange, baby blue, light pink,
turquoise, and periwinkle wool felt,
1¾ x 1¾ inches (4.4 x 4.4 cm) each

Rose, turquoise, hot pink, baby blue,
and light violet wool felt, 1 x 1 inch
(2.5 x 2.5 cm) each

Bright green, light green, turquoise,
and light pink wool felt scraps

Blue wool felt, 3½ x 3 inches
(8.9 x 7.6 cm) (for the bird)

Denim, 13 x 22 inches (33 x 55.9 cm)

Assorted shades of blue, green, pink,
red, and purple embroidery floss

Pillow insert, 12 x 18 inches
(30.5 x 45.7 cm)

WHAT YOU DO

1 Use the templates to cut one circle A from the hot pink, bright blue, medium pink, light blue, and lavender felt; one circle B from the orange, baby blue, light pink, turquoise, and periwinkle felt; and one circle C from the rose, turquoise, hot pink, baby blue, and light violet felt.

2 Layer three circles in descending size to create five flower heads in the following color combinations:

- hot pink, orange, and rose
- bright blue, baby blue, and turquoise
- medium pink, light pink, and hot pink
- light blue, turquoise, and baby blue
- lavender, periwinkle, and light violet

3 Referring to the photo for placement, baste the flower heads onto the yellow felt (be sure to leave room for the bird to sit atop the middle flower). Use the floss in contrasting colors to stitch down the circle flowers as shown in the photos and on the template, adding French knots (page 12) where the template indicates.

4 The leaves are all circles, half circles, or ovals. Use the templates to cut the following leaves for the flowers (going from left to right) and place beside their respective flowers for now:

- two ½-inch (1.3 cm) circles from bright green felt
- eleven ¼-inch (6 mm) circles from bright green felt
- four ½-inch (1.3 cm) ovals from the light green felt
- one ½-inch (1.3 cm) circle from light green felt, cut in half
- one ½-inch (1.3 cm) circle from bright green felt, cut in half, and one ¾-inch (1.9 cm) circle from bright green felt, cut in half

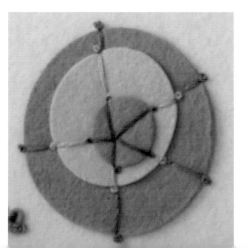

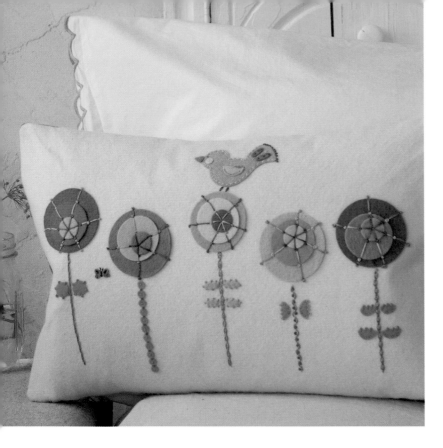

Stem Five (3¼ inches [8.3 cm] long): Use light and dark green floss and the double-threaded running stitch or the double-threaded backstitch. Hold the four leaves in place with light green floss and a straight stitch around the curve and French knots at the top edges.

6   Use the template to cut the bird shape from the blue felt, the beak from turquoise felt, one ¾-inch (1.9 cm) circle from bright green felt (then cut it in half to form the wing), one ¼-inch (6 mm) circle from light pink felt for the bird's cheek, and two ½-inch (1.3 cm) ovals from turquoise felt for the tail embellishments.

7   Using the photos for reference, assemble the bird. Then use floss in complementary colors and the backstitch to attach the bird, wing, and tail embellishments to the pillow front.

8   Make one French knot with black floss for the bird's eye. Add French knots with the purple floss to the blue oval tail embellishments and to make the dots at the end of the tail. Add French knots in green floss to the top right corner of the wing. Use floss in complementary colors to backstitch the pink cheek and beak to the bird. Don't forget to give your little birdie feet! A few straight stitches in dark purple floss should do it.

9   Make the butterfly by cutting two small heart shapes from turquoise felt and placing them, points together, between the first two flowers to form wings. Hold the wings in place with two hot pink French knots on each side. Make the butterfly body with three black French knots and use two black straight stitches for antenna.

10   The pillow is a simple envelope closure. To make it, cut the denim into one 13 x 10-inch (33 x 25.4 cm) piece and one 13 x 12-inch (33 x 30.5 cm) piece. Finish one 13-inch (33 cm) edge on each piece by turning it under ½ inch (1.3 cm) twice and sewing to hem. Place the yellow pillow front right-side-up on a work surface. Lay the larger denim piece right-side-down on top, aligning the three raw edges with the edges of the pillow front. Place the smaller denim piece, right-side-down on top of both pieces, again aligning the three raw edges with the edges of the pillow front. Pin the pieces together and sew along the four outside edges. Trim the corners, turn the whole thing right side out, insert a pillow, and you're done.

5   Going from left to right, embroider the stems and add the leaves as follows:

Stem One (4 inches [10.2 cm] long): Use the light and dark green floss and the single-threaded running stitch (page 12) or the single-threaded backstitch. Hold each leaf in place with six French knots in light green floss.

Stem Two (3¾ inches [9.5 cm] long): Use the light green floss and alternate French knots with ¼-inch (6 mm) bright green circles, held in place with another French knot.

Stem Three (3¾ inches [9.5 cm] long): Use light and dark green floss and the double-threaded running stitch (page 12) or the double-threaded backstitch. Hold each of the four oval leaves in place with six French knots in light green floss.

Stem Four (3 inches [7.6 cm] long): Use light and dark green floss and the single-threaded running stitch or the single threaded backstitch. Hold the two leaves in place with light green floss and a straight stitch around the curve and French knots at the edges.

Felty Family Portraits

What dad wouldn't love a felty family portrait? Use photographs and felt to make pictures of his loved ones.

Felty Family Portraits

DESIGNER: SUZIE MILLIONS

WHAT YOU NEED

(to make one)

Templates (page 126)

Basic sewing kit (page 9)

Craft knife

Straightedge

Poster board

Spray adhesive

Gray felt, about 7 x 8 inches (17.8 x 20.3 cm), for the frame

Fabric pen with disappearing ink (see note in step 3)

White thread

Felt for the background

Photo

Photocopier

Clear sheet protector, cut into 3 x 3-inch (7.6 x 7.6 cm) squares

Fine point permanent marker

Felt scraps in assorted colors, for hair, eyes, clothes, etc.

Toothpicks

Transparent tape

Double-sided tape

Bone folder

WHAT YOU DO

1 Copy and cut out the templates in the back of the book. Cut out the image opening in the center of the frame template. Using the templates, the craft knife, and the straightedge, cut one easel back from the poster board. Cut two 5 x 6-inch (12.7 x 15.2 cm) rectangles from the poster-board, but don't cut out the image opening in the center of either rectangle yet.

2 Lightly coat one 5 x 6-inch (12.7 x 15.2 cm) poster board rectangle with spray adhesive, and center the board on the back of the gray felt, smoothing gently to remove any wrinkles. Cut the excess felt from around the poster board, using a craft knife and straightedge, but still don't cut out the image-opening area yet.

Tip: Always use a very sharp blade and straightedge to cut felt, pressing down and advancing slowly. If you pull the knife too quickly, the felt will stretch and give you misshapen, fuzzy cuts. Protect your project from knife slips and nicks by placing the straightedge onto the project and cutting toward the scrap edge, not the project.

3 Lay the frame template on top of the felt panel you created in the last step, and use the fabric pen with disappearing ink to draw the image opening and the diagonal lines at each corner onto the felt. (Note: Make sure you use a fabric pen with ink that will disappear from your felt completely without having to use water.) The easiest way to get the woodgrain pattern onto the frame is to just draw it freehand onto the felt with the disappearing ink fabric pen, referring to the template or photograph. All wood is unique, so don't stress about making the grain markings perfect.

4 Use the white thread to free-motion stitch (page 10) the woodgrain pattern right through both the felt and the poster board. Trim all loose threads as you work. For a sharp turn, stop stitching with the needle below the felt and posterboard, lift the pressure foot, rotate the fabric, lower the foot, and begin stitching again. Sew the diagonal lines in each corner after you've stitched the woodgrain.

5 Now you can use the craft knife and straightedge to cut out the image opening in the center of the felt panel.

6 Cut a 3 x 4-inch (7.6 x 10.2 cm) piece of felt for the portrait's background—experiment to find a color that contrasts well with the hair color of your person or pet. To begin making your felt family member, use the portrait templates provided, customizing them as needed to capture a likeness, or make your own by tracing a photo you've enlarged or reduced to fit the frame opening. Use the squares of sheet protector material and a fine point marker to trace the hair, facial features, clothing, etc., to make templates. Simplify—crisp, basic shapes make these portraits fun.

7 Trace around the templates on the various felt scraps, and then cut out the pieces. Start by cutting the face, ears, shoulders, and neck. As you work, assemble the pieces on the background felt, but don't glue yet. Trim and adjust pieces as needed. Keep the frame front handy so you can lay it over your portrait as you progress to see what will show through the image opening. You can use a paper punch if you have one to make perfectly round pieces (great for eyes). Add wire, beads, embroidery floss, and other trims to make additional details.

8 Using white craft glue, assemble the portrait, gluing the bottom layer to the background, and then working your way up, gluing each layer to the layer below it. For very small pieces, pour glue on scrap paper and use a toothpick to apply the glue to the felt. Use clean toothpicks to position small pieces of felt.

9 Attach the felt portraits to the back of the stitched frames with the transparent tape, pressing firmly. Apply the double-sided tape to all four edges of one side of the blank piece of 5 x 6 inch (12.7 x 15.2 cm) poster board you set aside earlier, and press the piece firmly to the back of the stitched frame.

10 Use a bone folder to score along the dotted line of the easel back and crease. Apply double-sided tape to the full length of the easel back, align the bottom edge with the center of the bottom edge of the frame back, and press the easel firmly in place.

Celebrate Dad with these felt moustaches—they also make great props for fun family photos!

Manly Moustaches

DESIGNER: LAURA HOWARD

WHAT YOU NEED

Templates (page 122)

Basic sewing kit (page 9)

Felt in your chosen moustache color, 3 x 5 inches (7.6 x 12.7 cm)

Thread in a contrasting color

Thread in a matching color

Black or white hat elastic (or other narrow elastic)

WHAT YOU DO

1 Use the template to cut out three moustache pieces from your chosen felt color: two outer moustaches and one inner moustache.

2 Hold or pin the inner moustache shape to the back of one of the larger, outer shapes. Use a double thickness of the contrasting color thread to backstitch a decorative line around the front of the moustache, sewing the two layers together.

3 Cut a 20-inch (50 cm) length of the elastic. The elastic should be long enough to loop around the back of the intended moustache-wearer's head from one side of his (or her) mouth to the other.

4 Sew one end of the elastic onto one side of the plain outer moustache shape, so the elastic overlaps the felt by approximately ½ inch (1.3 cm). Use the whipstitch in matching thread to sew it in place, then loop the elastic (taking care not to twist it), and sew the other end to the other side of the moustache.

5 Hold or pin the front and back moustache pieces together, so the ends of the elastic are sandwiched between them. Use the matching sewing thread to whipstitch around the edges, finishing your stitching neatly at the back.

Here's a no-sew project so simple even kids can make it. Raid your recycling bin for cardboard tubes and cereal boxes!

Rockets' Red Glare

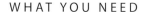

DESIGNER: KATHY SHELDON

WHAT YOU NEED

Template (see step 3)

Basic sewing kit (page 9)

Scrap paper

Cardboard tubes of various sizes

Red, navy blue, and blue felt sheets

Ribbons, an assortment of red, white, and blue in stars, stripes, and polka dots

Blue rickrack

Cardstock

Stapler or tape (optional)

Red and blue embroidery floss

WHAT YOU DO

1 Wrap the scrap paper around the cardboard tube, then cut it so it fits the top and bottom of the tube exactly and overlaps at the edges by about ½ inch (1.3 cm). Use this as a template to cut the felt to cover the tube.

2 Adhere the felt to the tube with fabric glue and smooth any wrinkles. Decorate by gluing on the ribbons and/or rickrack.

3 Enlarge or reduce one of the circle templates from the back of the book as needed for the size of your tube—it doesn't have to be exact, just be sure you'll have some overhang once the circle becomes a cone on top of the tube. Use this template to cut a circle out of cardstock (or a cereal box). Cover one side of the cardstock circle with glue, and adhere it to a piece of felt. Cut out the circle, leaving a just a bit of a felt edge showing around the outside of the cardstock.

4 Cut a line straight into the center of the felt-covered circle. Overlap the cut edges to form a cone that fits over the top of your tube with a bit of overhang. Once the size of the cone is right, secure the edges with glue, tape, or a stapler. If gluing, let dry completely.

5 Cut lengths of ribbon so they're long enough to fit through the tube and trail down nicely. Cut about 1 yard (.9 m) of the embroidery floss (longer or shorter depending on where you want to hang your rocket), and tie the ribbons to one end of the floss. Thread a large needle onto the other end, poke the threaded needle through the center of your covered cone, then pull the floss all the way through.

6 Drop the ribbons down through the felt-covered tube, and then coat the very top edge of the tube with fabric glue. Press the cone cover down onto the tube, and let the glue dry completely before hanging your rocket.

Indoors for brunch or outdoors on a porch, celebrate the 4th in style with this bunting of red, white, and blue.

July 4th Bunting

DESIGNER: CONSTANÇA CABRAL

WHAT YOU NEED

(to make a bunting about 5 yards [4.6 m] long)

Templates (page 118)

Basic sewing kit (page 9)

White, red, and blue felt, each 18 x 22 inches (45.7 x 55.9 cm)

Fabric scraps in red, white, and blue featuring polka dots, stripes, stars, etc.

White thread

Wool needle (must have a big eye and be relatively sharp)

6 yards (5.5 m) of red and white baker's twine

WHAT YOU DO

1 Using the template, cut 15 large triangles, five of each color from the felt—use a rotary cutter or fabric scissors, not pinking shears, to cut these pieces.

2 Using the template, cut 15 small fabric triangles from your various fabric scraps, again using a rotary cutter or fabric scissors.

3 Now you get to use your pinking shears, but only to scallop the two sides of each fabric triangle; leave the top of each fabric triangle straight for now.

4 Place one small fabric triangle on top of one large felt triangle, making sure to align the top edges. Repeat for all the pairs of triangles. Press each pair using a hot iron to make the triangles stick to each other—this makes the next step much easier.

5 Use white thread to stitch around the entire inside perimeter of the small triangle, being careful to follow two different seam allowances: use a ¼-inch (6 mm) seam allowance when

sewing the sides, and a ½-inch (1.3 cm) seam allowance when sewing the tops. Trim all the threads and press again.

6 Cut all around the finished double triangle with your pinking shears. This means you'll now be cutting only the felt on the sides and the combined felt and fabric on the tops. Don't cut away too much—simply trim out the edges, leaving plenty of seam allowance.

7 Thread the wool needle with the baker's twine. Leave approximately 15 inches (38.1 cm) of twine, then tie a knot and then use a running stitch (½-inch [1.3 cm] stitches look nice) to stitch across the top of the triangle. Tie a knot in the twine to prevent the triangle from moving along the bunting.

8 Leave a 4-inch (10.2 cm) length of twine, then tie a knot and start stitching another triangle. Repeat for all triangles, alternating the colors and always leaving a 4-inch (10.2 cm) length of baker's twine between triangles. Don't forget to tie knots at the beginning and end of each triangle. When you're done, leave a 15-inch (38.1 cm) length.

Avast, matey!
In 1995, September 19th
was officially declared
Talk Like a Pirate Day.
This parrot and eyepatch
will turn you from
landlubber to scallywag
in no time.

Yo Ho Ho Pirate Parrot

DESIGNER: LAURA HOWARD

WHAT YOU NEED

(for the parrot)

Templates (page 124)

Basic sewing kit (page 9)

Red felt, 9 x 22 inches (22.9 x 55.9 cm)

White felt, 2 x 2½ inches (5.1 x 6.4 cm)

Black felt, a small scrap

Blue felt, 3½ x 4 inches (8.9 x 10.2 cm)

Yellow felt, 3½ x 4 inches (8.9 x 10.2 cm)

Thread in colors to match felt

1 or 2 pin backs

WHAT YOU DO

(to make the parrot)

1 Cut out the following pieces using the templates provided: three red parrots, one red wing, one red feather piece; one white face; one black eye, one black lower beak; one blue tail, one blue feather piece; one yellow upper beak, one yellow feather piece, one yellow left foot, and one yellow right foot.

2 Using the photo for reference, use the running stitch and matching colors of thread to sew all the small pieces onto one of the red parrot shapes in the following order: the two beak pieces, the face, the eye, the feet, the tail, and the wing. Then layer the three feather pieces onto the wing (blue first, then yellow, then red) and sew them all in place. (For extra neatness, you can also whipstitch over the inside edge of the wing to match the whipstitching you'll do around the edge of the parrot in step 4.) Trim any excess red felt showing around the edges.

3 Turn one of the plain red parrot pieces over, and sew one or two pin backs to the bottom using a double thickness of red thread.

4 Place the front and back parrot pieces together, sandwiching the third red parrot between them. Pin the layers together and whipstitch the edges. Use red thread to sew around the edge in one go or use matching threads to stitch it together section by section. If you use matching threads, start with the yellow feet and work counterclockwise, finishing with the red front of the parrot. Finish your stitching inside the layers to keep things neat, then finish the final bit of red stitching on the back.

5 To make a smaller parrot brooch instead, copy the pattern pieces at half the size required for the large parrot, and cut just one red parrot shape and no hat pieces. Sew the red parrot shape onto a 5 x 7-inch (12.7 x 17.8 cm) piece of white felt, using the whipstitch and red thread. Use matching threads to whipstitch all the smaller pieces in position. Cut around the parrot, leaving a small border of white felt around the edge. Use this shape as a template to cut a backing shape of white felt. Sew a pin back to the backing felt, then whipstitch the front and back together with white thread.

Templates (page 124)

**Black felt, 3½ x 4 inches
(8.9 x 10.2 cm)**

A scrap of white felt

White and black thread

White and black embroidery floss

(for the eyepatch)

Templates (page 124)

Black felt, 2¾ x 4¾ inches (7 x 12 cm)

White felt, 2 x 2½ inches (5.1 x 6.4 cm)

Black and white sewing thread

2 black seed beads

Black hat elastic or other narrow elastic, up to 21 inches (53.3 cm)

(to make the parrot's hat)

1 Use the templates to cut out two black hat shapes and one white hat skull shape.

2 Using the photo for reference, position the skull on one of the hat shapes, leaving room to stitch the bones below it. Sew it in place using the whipstitch and the white thread.

3 Backstitch two bones under the skull using a large needle and the white embroidery floss. Make each bone by stitching one long line and adding two stitches in a V shape at each end.

4 Divide a six-strand length of the black embroidery floss into three strands and sew a small cross of two stitches for each eye and a backstitched line with four stitches across it for the mouth.

5 Pin or hold the two hat pieces together, and sew around the edges with the whipstitch and black thread, leaving the bottom edge open. Position the hat on the parrot's head at an angle and sew along the bottom with the running stitch in more black thread to sew it in place. Finish your stitching at the back.

Tip: If you'd like to make a pirate's hat brooch, follow steps 1 through 4, then sew a pin back onto the backing hat piece with a double thickness of black thread. Sew the front and back together with more black thread, whipstitching around all the edges.

(to make the eyepatch)

1 Cut out two black eyepatch shapes, one white skull shape, and two white bones.

2 Cut two narrow triangles from the top of each eyepatch shape, using the dotted lines on the templates as a guide. Using black thread, whipstitch the edges of each triangle-shaped opening together to give each patch a three-dimensional shape. Be sure to sew the back of one piece and the front of the other so your stitching will be hidden between the pieces when they're sewn together.

3 Arrange the skull and bones on the center of the front eyepatch piece. Hold them in place and sew around them using the whipstitch and white thread. Sew around the skull first—the bones will be held into position at the same time, ensuring the whole design doesn't slip as you sew.

4 Stitch a mouth on the skull using black thread by backstitching a line across the bottom of the skull then sewing four vertical stitches across it.

5 Use black thread to sew two black seed beads in position for the eyes. Sew the beads so they lie flat (like an O) by adding three or four stitches.

6 For an adult-sized eyepatch, cut an approximately 21-inch (53.3 cm) length of the narrow black elastic. For smaller eyepatches, cut the elastic to fit the intended wearer (if you're making an eyepatch for a child, remember these are not toys, and children should always be supervised when wearing them).

7 Sew the elastic to the back piece of the eyepatch—the ends of the elastic should overlap the felt by about ⅝ inch (1.6 cm), and the elastic should be sewn on at a slight diagonal angle as pictured. Use the whipstitch and black sewing thread to sew the elastic in place, taking care not to twist it when you sew the second end in position.

8 Pin or hold the front and back pieces together and sew around the edges with the whipstitch and black thread. Finish your stitching neatly at the back.

This project will transform a plain shirt into a cute flying creature in a few quick steps, and it's adjustable to just about any size.

Bat Costume

DESIGNER: ELLEN LUCKETT BAKER

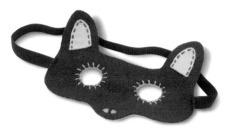

WHAT YOU NEED

Templates (page 114)

Basic sewing kit (page 9)

Long-sleeved brown x-small T-shirt

Brown wool felt, 1 yard (.9 m) in a shade to match the T-shirt (for wings)

Brown felt, 5 x 8 inches (12.7 x 20.3 cm) (for the mask)

Pink felt, 4 x 4 inches (10.2 x 10.2 cm) (for the insides of the ears)

¼-inch (6 mm) boning, 1 yard (.9 m) (available at fabric stores)

Brown thread

Heavyweight fusible interfacing, 5 x 8 inches (12.7 x 20.3 cm)

Fabric glue

Light brown embroidery floss

Brown embroidery floss

½-inch (1.3 cm) elastic, 15 inches (38.1 cm)

WHAT YOU DO

(to make the body)

1 Use the template to cut two wings from the yard (.9 m) of brown felt—adjust the size of the wings to fit your size T-shirt by measuring your shirt from armpit to sleeve end and then from armpit to bottom hem, and adjusting the wing size to match.

2 For each wing, measure from point a to point b, and then measure from point c to point d, using the template for reference. Use these measurements to cut two lengths of boning and two 1-inch-wide (2.5 cm) strips of brown felt. You should have four strips of boning and four strips of felt for two wings.

3 On the back of one wing, pin a boning strip from point a to point b. Place a felt strip on top of the boning, and sew both in place along either side of the strip. (Be sure that your bobbin thread matches the felt color.) Repeat to attach the boning and felt from point c to point d. Now repeat this step for the other wing.

4 Next, pin one wing along the side and sleeve seams of the T-shirt. Sew the wing to the shirt with a ⅛-inch (3 mm) seam allowance. Repeat for the other wing.

How each wing attaches to the shirt

(to make the mask)

1 Press the 5 x 8-inch (12.7 x 20.3 cm) piece of heavyweight fusible interfacing to the back side of the 5 x 8-inch (12.7 x 20.3 cm) piece of brown felt.

2 Use the template to cut the mask from the fused felt and interfacing. Fold over to cut the eyeholes. Cut the pink felt for the inside of the ears.

3 Use the fabric glue to attach the insides of the ears to the mask, and then stitch around their perimeter, using the brown floss and the running stitch.

4 Use the satin stitch and the light brown floss to make the nostrils, and stitch around the eyeholes with the blanket stitch.

5 Fold over one end of the elastic, and machine stitch it to one side of the back of the mask. If possible, adjust the fit around the child's head, and then stitch the other end of the elastic to the mask in the same manner.

Halloweenie Bag

Halloweenie and his best friend, Jack, will deliver up a bagful of treats (and maybe a trick or two—these guys can be sneaky!).

Halloweenie Bag

DESIGNER: CATHY GAUBERT

WHAT YOU NEED

Templates (page 117)

Basic sewing kit (page 9)

Lavender felt in the following sizes:

- Two 6 x 8-inch (15.2 x 20.3 cm) pieces (front and back of bag)

- Two 4 x 8-inch (10.2 x 20.3 cm) pieces (sides of bag)

- One 4 x 6-inch (10.2 x 15.2 cm) piece (bottom of bag)

Green felt, 4 x 11 inches (10.2 x 27.9 cm)

Black felt, 3 x 3 inches (7.6 x 7.6 cm)

Orange felt, 2½ x 2½ inch (6.4 x 6.4 cm) piece

White felt, about ¼ x 8-inch (6 mm x 20.3 cm) strip

Patterned fabric, 24 x 8 inches (61 x 20.3 cm), plus scrap for party hat

Iron-on adhesive, 24 x 8 inches (61 x 20.3 cm), plus scrap for party hat

2 mismatched buttons

Gray and green thread

Green embroidery floss

WHAT YOU DO

1   Cut the lavender felt into five rectangles, following the sizes listed in What You Need. Use the manufacturer's directions to adhere the iron-on adhesive to the patterned fabric. Then cut the patterned fabric into five rectangles to match the five felt rectangles, but don't remove the paper backing. Set all felt and fabric rectangles aside for now.

2   Using the templates, cut Halloweenie's head and wings and Jack's eyes from the black felt. From the green felt, cut Halloweenie's body, Jack's stem, and two 1 x 11-inch (2.5 x 27.9 cm) strips for the handles. From the orange felt, cut the pumpkin shape (Jack!) and Halloweenie's nose. From the white felt strip, cut three 2-inch-long (5.1 cm) pieces for Halloweenie's two legs and Jack's grin. Cut a strip about 1¾-inches (4.4 cm) long for Halloweenie's grin. Or just snip away… you'll make it work!

3   Use a dab of fabric glue to adhere the felt pieces (except for the eyes and grins) to the front felt panel of the bag (refer to the photos for placement). With gray thread and your machine set to a straight stitch, sew just a bit inside the edge of each felt piece (head, wings, body, nose, and pumpkin).

4   For the legs, set your stitch to zigzag (you may have to adjust the width and length) and sew directly on top of each leg to create Halloweenie's stripey tights. Use this same procedure for each fellow's grin. Trim the felt flush with the sides of their faces.

5 Use the template to cut the party hat from the scrap of patterned fabric with adhesive backing. Place it atop Halloweenie's head, and iron and then stitch it in place.

6 Attach one of Jack's felt eyes with an X stitch and one with a few satin stitches.

7 Machine stitch a little triangle nose for Jack, and attach his stem with a straight stitch.

8 Now iron each adhesive-backed fabric panel to the corresponding felt panel, following the manufacturer's directions.

9 With fabric sides facing, stitch the bag parts together in the following order: front panel to one side panel, to back panel, to the other side panel, to front panel.

10 With fabric sides facing, pin the bottom panel to the bag. Stand the bag up on your sewing machine, and carefully

stitch around the base to attach it to the bag. Topstitch around the top of the bag before adding the handles.

11 To make the handles, fold each green strip in half lengthwise, thread your machine with the green thread, and stitch along the edges with green thread. Refer to the photos for placement, and attach the handles by stitching an X.

12 Sew the mismatched button eyes onto Halloweenie's face with green thread.

Each year, the
Great Mini Pumpkins
rise out of the
pumpkin patch.
When these land,
you can use them
as pincushions.

Great Mini Pumpkins

DESIGNER: CATHY ZIEGELE

WHAT YOU NEED

Templates (page 122)

Basic sewing kit (page 9)

**Orange felt, 4¹/₂ x 12 inches
(11.4 x 30.5 cm)**

Green felt, 4 x 4 inches (10.2 x 10.2 cm)

Brown felt, 1 x 2¹/₄ inches (2.5 x 5.7 cm)

9 inches (22.9 cm) of green floral wire

**Brown, green, and orange
embroidery floss**

Polyfill

Rice or navy beans

WHAT YOU DO

1 Use the templates to cut six panels for the pumpkin body from the orange felt, and two leaf shapes from the green felt. Set aside.

2 Fold the floral wire about 3 inches (7.6 cm) from one end (so it looks like a check mark), and make a flat knot at the top of the short end of the fold. Lay the folded wire on top of the brown strip of felt (this will be the stem). Roll the felt stem with the wire on top from one end, just like rolling a jellyroll. Be sure to keep the wire knot and stem extending from the rolled felt. Sew the stem closed with the brown embroidery floss.

3 Use the blanket stitch and the green floss to sew the front and back of the leaf together around the wire knot, making sure to fully enclose the wire.

4 Curl the floral wire stem around a wood skewer to shape it.

5 Use the blanket stitch and orange floss to sew two panel pieces together—the blanket stitch will be on the outside of the pumpkin. Sew three sets of two panels

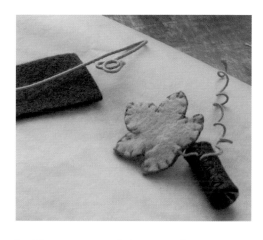

in this manner, and then sew the sets together, but leave one section about half open so you can stuff the pumpkin after the stem is in.

6 Insert the stem and leaf Into the top of the assembled pumpkin, and sew it with orange floss to anchor it securely to the top of the pumpkin.

7 Stuff the pumpkin with polyfill. Be sure to place the fill around the stem so the stem stands straight. Once you have about three-fourths of the pumpkin stuffed, add a few ounces of rice or beans for weight on the bottom, and finish stuffing with a thin layer of stuffing. Sew the pumpkin closed and you are done!

Yum! Tuck a name card between the whipped cream and the crust and you can use these pie slices as place card holders.

(Pumpkin) Pie in the Sky

DESIGNER: AIMEE RAY

WHAT YOU NEED

Templates (page 127)

Basic sewing kit (page 9)

Pumpkin orange, tan, and cream felt, 9 x 12 inches (22.9 x 30.5 cm) each

Brown embroidery floss

White, orange, and tan thread

Stuffing

WHAT YOU DO

1 Using the templates, cut two side pieces and one top piece from the pumpkin orange felt. Cut one bottom piece and one crust piece from the tan felt. Cut one whipped cream piece from the cream felt.

2 To embroider the swirl designs on each side piece, first trace the embroidery pattern onto the tissue paper, and then pin it securely in place onto the felt piece. Embroider the designs through both the tissue paper and the felt, using the brown floss and the lazy daisy (page 11) and split stitch page (12). Tear away the tissue paper. You may need to use a needle or tweezers to pull out little pieces from underneath your stitches.

3 To make the whipped cream, use the white thread to make a stitch in each top corner

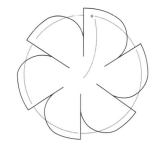

and then gather the thread together (see below). Pull the thread down through the center of the circle and tie a knot underneath. Stitch this piece onto the top pie piece.

4 Stitch the top, sides, and bottom pie pieces together using the whipstitch and the orange thread. Stuff the pie firmly, but not enough so the sides bulge. Stitch on the back crust piece using the whipstitch and the tan thread.

These felted wool coasters coordinate nicely with the Autumn Leaves Table Runner (page 84).

Autumn Leaves Coasters

DESIGNER: LISA JORDAN

WHAT YOU NEED

Template (page 121)

Basic sewing kit (page 9)

**Felted garment wool (page 8)
or wool felt in autumn colors**

**Felt for backing (felted garment wool,
wool felt, or eco felt would all work)**

**Embroidery floss in contrasting
and matching colors**

Jute twine

WHAT YOU DO

1 Use the template to cut one leaf shape from the felted garment wool or wool felt and one leaf shape from the backing felt for each coaster.

2 Divide a six-strand length of embroidery floss in a contrasting color into three strands, and begin stitching the decorative veining on the leaves. Begin by stitching the center vein first, followed by the radial veins.

3 Cut a 3-inch-long (7.6 cm) piece of the jute twine, make a short loop, and knot the end.

4 Position the stitched leaf on top of its backing, sandwiching the jute loop between the two pieces of fabric at the top. Tack the leaves in place with fabric glue if desired.

5 Choose a color of floss that matches the top of the leaf, and stitch the two pieces together using the blanket stitch. Start stitching at the top of the leaf, securing the knot of the jute loop beneath the stitches. Continue stitching around the outside of the leaf, concealing the knot inside the stitching when finished.

Bring the ambience
of autumn indoors
with this leaf-strewn
table runner.

Autumn Leaves Table Runner

DESIGNER: LISA JORDAN

WHAT YOU NEED

Template (page 113)

Basic sewing kit (page 9)

Burlap fabric (sized to fit your table)

Brown felt yardage, 2 inches (5.1 cm) wider and longer than the burlap (for the base of the runner)

Wool felt, felted garment wool (page 8), or eco felt in assorted autumn colors (for leaves)

Embroidery floss in autumn colors that contrast with your felt

Thread, in a color to match the burlap

WHAT YOU DO

1 Cut the burlap to the size desired for your table runner, leaving it 1 inch (2.5 cm) longer and wider than your intended size to allow for fraying. Set it aside. If you haven't already done so, cut the brown felt 2 inches (5.1 cm) longer and wider than the intended size of your burlap, and set it aside.

2 Cut the leaf shapes from your various colors of felt using the template provided. The number of leaves you'll need will depend on the size of your runner and just how leaf-strewn you'd like it to look.

3 Use three strands of floss to stitch the veining on the leaves. Start by stitching the four sets of radial veins in an upside down V formation—don't stitch the center vein yet (that vein will attach the leaves to the runner). Stitch the first V at the widest part of the leaf using the running stitch: start in the middle of the V and sew towards the leaf's edge. Work your thread back to the center on the underside of the leaf by wrapping around your stitches as if using the single-threaded running stitch (page 12).

4 Sew down the other side of the V and back to center, again wrapping your stitches. Vary the tension on the thread so the leaf buckles slightly, adding dimension. Repeat this process for the other Vs on the leaf, and knot the thread in an inconspicuous place when finished.

5 Repeat this process with the other leaves, making some flat and some more dimensional.

6 Lay out your burlap and plan where you'll place your leaves. Scatter the leaves randomly across the runner or arrange them in a design of your choosing—if you'll be using the runner functionally, leave leafless places to set pots and pans or plates. You'll be sewing around the burlap, so do keep your leaves at least ¾ inch (1.9 cm) from the edge of the burlap.

7 Thread your needle with three strands of the same color embroidery floss you used for the Vs, and stitch the leaf's center vein to the burlap using the running stitch. Knot the floss beneath the burlap. Repeat this process until your runner is as leafy as you like.

8 Center the leaf-covered burlap on the length of brown felt and pin it into place. Use a sewing machine and the burlap-color thread to stitch the burlap to the brown felt using a short to medium zigzag stitch, about a ½ inch (1.3 cm) from the edge of the burlap. If your burlap has frayed a lot, be sure to stitch inside the frayed area. Trim the edges of the burlap. For a neater look, gently pull out any loose threads of burlap running outside of, and parallel to, your stitching.

Tip: Clean up any stray burlap fibers with a lint roller or sticky tape.

Happy Hanukkah Mice

These little mice are looking for a dreidel to spin and some Hanukkah gelt to nibble.

Happy Hanukkah Mice

DESIGNER: KATHY SHELDON

WHAT YOU NEED

(to make the girl mouse)

Templates (page 118)

Basic sewing kit (page 9)

Light gray and blue felt

Black, white, and gray embroidery floss

WHAT YOU DO

1 Using a fabric pen, transfer the following templates to the gray felt: two each of the head, body, and ear shapes, and one of the tail shape. Transfer the dress shape onto the blue felt. Don't cut the shapes out yet because it's easier to embroider on larger pieces of felt.

2 Use two strands of the black embroidery floss to add two French knots for the eyes (page 12) to one face outline. Trace the Star of David design onto tissue paper, and pin it securely in place on the dress outline. Embroider with two strands of the white embroidery floss and simple stitches, following the over and under pattern. Gently tear away the tissue paper.

3 Cut out all of the pieces.

4 Align the two body pieces and then add the dress, with the embroidery side facing up. Use the one strand of gray embroidery floss and the running stitch to begin sewing all the pieces together, starting at the right bottom edge of the body. Stop, but don't tie off the floss, when you get to the top of the right shoulder.

5 Add the two head pieces, with the bottom of the face just overlapping the top of the body and the bottom of the back head piece just overlapping the back of the body. Continue stitching up the right side to attach the two head pieces until you get to where the bottom of the ear would go—stop again, but don't tie off the floss.

6 Fold over the top corner of one ear, and tuck the ear between the front and back head pieces. Continue stitching to attach the ear, and stitch all the way over to the left until you get to where the top of the second ear will go. Repeat this step to attach the second ear.

7 Stitch the rest of the head and tie off, hiding your knot between the two felt head pieces. Then stitch down the other side of the body, again attaching the dress at the same time.

8 Stitch the tail to the back of the body.

9 Use two strands of black floss to make a French knot for the nose at the very bottom of the mouse's head. Thread a needle with three strands of white embroidery floss, and poke it behind the nose, pulling until you have plenty of floss on either side for whiskers. Cut the white floss, and tie it in a tight little knot that's hidden behind the nose. Trim the floss if needed, and separate the pieces of floss with the tip of a needle.

Simple but adorable—
that's what we call
the perfect felt
Christmas ornament!

Christmas Ornaments

DESIGNER: AIMEE RAY

WHAT YOU NEED

(to make one ornament)

Templates and embroidery patterns (page 123)

Basic sewing kit (page 9)

Felt in festive colors

Patterned fabric, optional

Embroidery floss in contrasting colors

Stuffing

Satin ribbon, 5 inches (12.7 cm)

WHAT YOU DO

1 Using the templates, cut two circles of felt. It's fun to use different colors for each side or to use patterned fabric for the back. Use pinking shears instead of regular scissors for a fancy edge.

2 Trace the embroidery pattern onto tissue paper, and pin it securely in place on the front felt piece. Embroider the design (through both felt and paper).

3 Tear away the tissue paper. You may need to use a needle or tweezers to pull out pieces from underneath your stitches.

4 Pin the two pieces of each ornament together, wrong sides facing. Hiding the knot inside, begin stitching 1/4 inch (6 mm) in around the edge with embroidery floss. Tuck a bit of stuffing inside along with the two ends of the piece of ribbon to make a loop. Finish embroidering and hide your end knot on the inside.

This is a "do it while you watch TV or listen to the radio" kind of project—it takes some time, but the results are worth it (especially when you stand beneath it with someone you love)!

Mistletoe Kissing Ball

DESIGNER: AMANDA CARESTIO

no sew

WHAT YOU NEED

Templates (page 122)

Basic sewing kit (page 9)

Green felt (for flower petals)

Red felt (for flower centers)

Foam sphere, 6 inches (15.2 cm) in diameter

Straight pins

Green gingham ribbon, 10 inches (25.4 cm)

WHAT YOU DO

1 Cut 3-inch-wide (7.6 cm) strips from the green felt. Fold one strip in half width-wise, and place the flower petal template on the fold. Pin in place or trace, and cut out each flower shape. You'll need about 200 to 250 flowers.

2 Trace the flower center template shape onto the red felt and cut out. You'll need as many flower centers as you have flowers.

3 Stack one flower center on top of one flower petal shape, and place it on the foam sphere. Stick a pin through the center.

4 Continue adding flowers around the entire felt shape, layering and overlapping the flowers as you go.

5 Fold the ribbon in half. Find a spot between two flowers, and pin the ribbon ends to the foam sphere, using several pins for added strength.

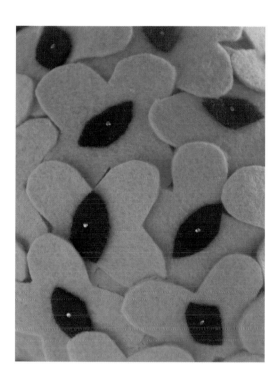

These jolly fellows would make a great gift or would be happy to lend some holiday cheer to your mantel.

Merry Little Bowling Elves

DESIGNER: ELLEN LUCKETT BAKER

WHAT YOU NEED

(for six elves):

Templates (page 113)

Basic sewing kit (page 9)

Green wool felt, 1/2 yard (.5 m)

Tan wool felt, 1/4 yard (.2 m)

Red and white striped cotton, 1/4 yard (.2 m)

Brown embroidery floss

Red embroidery floss

Matching thread

1 bag of polyfill stuffing

1 chopstick

Funnel

Dry rice, 3 cups (.63 kg)

6 jingle bells

WHAT YOU DO

1 Use the templates to cut all the parts from the felt and the striped cotton. For six elves, you will need 12 head pieces, 12 upper body pieces, 12 lower body pieces, 12 ears, and 6 hats.

2 Either draw eyes and a mouth centered on one head piece of felt freehand with a fabric marker, or trace the eyes and mouth on the template onto tissue paper and pin it securely in place onto the felt piece. Embroider the design (through both felt and tissue paper if tracing) using the satin stitch and the brown floss for the eyes and the running stitch and the red floss for the mouth. Repeat for all six elves.

3 Place the ears and one embroidered head piece right sides together, with the ears positioned over the face for now. Then machine baste the ears to the side of the head piece 1/8 inch (3 mm) from the edge. Repeat this step for all six elves.

4 With right sides together, sew the head piece to the upper body piece using a 1/4-inch (6 mm) seam allowance. Repeat for all 12 body front and back pieces.

5 Next, sew each of these assembled pieces to a lower body piece, again positioning the fabric and felt with right sides together and using a ¼-inch (6 mm) seam allowance. Repeat for all 12 body front and back pieces. Press all seams open.

6 Pin a front and back body piece right sides together, and stitch around the outer edges, making sure the ears are tucked inside the head pieces, and leaving a 2-inch (5.1 cm) opening at the bottom. Now you'll need to square off the bottom corners to create a box shape that will allow the elves to stand upright. Pull the felt apart at one corner, and flatten it out so that the seam is on the top. Insert this corner under your presser foot and sew, just about ¾ inch (1.9 cm) from the tip. Trim off the corner and sew with an overcasting stitch. Repeat for all of the bottom corners.

7 Turn one elf right side out and stuff with polyfill until almost full, poking with the chopstick to ensure that the filling is packed tightly. Then, using the funnel, fill up the bottom portion of the elf with ¼ to ½ cup (52.2 to 105 g) of dry rice. Sew the bottom closed by hand. Repeat for all elves.

8 Now fold each hat piece in half and sew along the long edge to form a cone. Turn the hat right side out, and poke out the top of the hat using the chopstick. Use a needle and thread to securely sew a jingle bell to each hat. (See Safety Note page 10.)

9 Glue one hat to each elf's head, or you can stitch the hats in place.

Kinara Felt Board

Even the youngest children can add candles and "light" this felt kinara to celebrate Kwanzaa.

Kinara Felt Board

no sew

DESIGNER: KATHY SHELDON

WHAT YOU NEED

Templates (page 120)

Basic sewing kit (page 9)

Brown felt, 8½ x 6 inches
(21.6 x 15.2 cm)

Scraps of green, red, black,
yellow, and orange felt

Cream felt, 12 x 36 inches
(30.5 x 91.4 cm)

Brown, green, red, black,
and orange thread

WHAT YOU DO

1 Use the templates to cut one kinara shape from the brown felt, three short candles from the green felt, three short candles from the red felt, and one tall candle from the black felt. Cut seven large flame shapes from the yellow felt and seven small flames shapes from the orange felt.

2   Because felt doesn't fray, you can leave the edges of pieces unfinished, but for a more polished look, machine stitch in matching thread around the outside edges of the kinara and candles, then stitch decorative lines on the kinara and the small oval at the top of each candle. Trim all threads.

3   Center an orange flame on top of each yellow flame, and use your sewing machine to attach the two with a short line of red stitches. Trim all threads.

4   Fold the cream felt in half to form a 12 x 18-inch (30.5 x 45.7 cm) rectangle, with the fold on the top. With the red thread still in your sewing machine, zigzag stitch around the perimeter of the rectangle, leaving room at the top (where the fold is) for a dowel or branch to fit through. Trim all threads and your kinara is ready to hang and light!

Lighting the Kwanzaa Kinara

Kwanzaa is a weeklong festival celebrating African American heritage and culture that runs from December 26th until January 1st each year. Each lighting of the kinara represents one of the Kwanzaa's seven principles, or *Nguzo Saba*.

Day One: Light the black candle; it represents *Umoja* (oo-MOH-jah): Unity.

Day Two: Light the black candle and then the farthest red candle on the left. This represents the *Kujichagulia* (koo-jee-chah-goo-LEE-ah): Self-determination.

Day Three: Light the black candle, then the farthest red on the left, and then the farthest green candle on the right. This represents *Ujima* (oo-JEE-mah): Collective work and responsibility.

Day Four: Light the black candle, then the farthest red on the left, and then the farthest green on the right, then the next red on the left. This represents *Ujamaa* (oo-jah-MAH): Collective economics.

Day Five: Light the black candle, then the farthest red on the left, the farthest green on right, the next red, and then the next green. This represents *Nia* (NEE-ah): Purpose.

Day Six: Light the black candle, then the farthest red on the left, the farthest green on the right, the next red, the next green, and then the final red candle. This represents *Kuumba* (koo-OOM-bah): Creativity.

Day Seven: Light the black candle, then the farthest red on the left, the farthest green on the right, the next red candle, the next green, the final red and then the final green candle. This represents *Imani* (ee-MAH-nee): Faith.

Does this crown just scream happy or what? It ties in the back, so it will fit just about any age child or adult.

Happy Birthday Crown

DESIGNER: CYNTHIA SHAFFER

WHAT YOU NEED

Templates (page 119)

Basic sewing kit (page 9)

Decoupage medium

Book text, 1 page

Turquoise blue felt, 20 x 8 inches (50.8 x 20.3 cm)

Heavyweight nonwoven interfacing, 20 x 8 inches (50.8 x 20.3 cm)

Polka dot cotton fabric, 20 x 8 inches (50.8 x 20.3 cm)

Temporary spray adhesive

Turquoise and green thread

Scraps of yellow and orange felt

Scraps of green striped fabric (or any coordinating fabric)

6 white buttons

Yellow embroidery thread

¼-inch-wide (6 mm) orange satin ribbon, 48 inches (121.9 cm)

WHAT YOU DO

1 Apply a coat of the decoupage medium to the book text and let it dry, then flip it over and apply a coat to the back. Set it aside to dry.

2 Use the template to cut one crown shape from the turquoise felt, one from the heavyweight nonwoven interfacing, and one from the polka dot fabric.

3 Use the temporary spray adhesive to sandwich the interfacing between the felt and the polka dot fabric. Use the turquoise thread to sew around the entire outer edge of the crown ⅛ inch (3 mm) in. Sew one more line ¼ inch (6 mm) in from the bottom edge.

4 Cut a ½ x 18½-inch (1.3 x 47 cm) strip from the decoupaged book text. Use spray adhesive to adhere the strip to the lower portion of the crown, approximately 1 inch (2.5 cm) from the bottom edge. Sew the book text strip in place with the green thread.

5 Use the larger circle template to cut a total of seven circles from the yellow and orange felt and the green striped fabric, and 14 circles from the heavyweight interfacing. Set seven of the interfacing circles aside for now.

10 Arrange the white buttons on the crown, as shown in the photo, and use two strands of the yellow embroidery thread to sew them very securely in place, leaving tails of embroidery thread. Tie the floss in a knot and then trim the ends down to ½ inch (1.3 cm).

11 Cut four 12-inch (30.5 cm) lengths of the orange ribbon. Pin the ribbon to the inside back edge of the crown, one ribbon ½ inch (1.3 cm) from the top edge and one ribbon ½ inch (1.3 cm) from the lower edge, then repeat for the other side. Machine stitch in place.

6 Use spray adhesive to adhere each felt or fabric circle to an interfacing circle. Then use spray adhesive to adhere the combined circles to the strip of text on the crown. Use the photos for placement.

7 Using the green thread, free-motion stitch (page 10) in a swirl pattern inside the circles.

8 Use the larger circle template to cut seven circles from the turquoise felt. Use spray adhesive to sandwich the tips of the crown between the remaining interfacing circles you cut in step 5 and the turquoise felt circles.

9 Use the smaller circle template to cut out seven circles from the book text. Use spray adhesive to adhere the text circles to the turquoise circles. Use green thread to free-motion stitch in a swirl pattern.

Cake Toppers

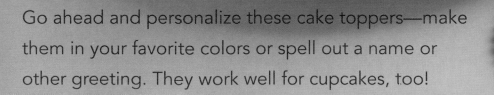

Go ahead and personalize these cake toppers—make them in your favorite colors or spell out a name or other greeting. They work well for cupcakes, too!

Cake Toppers

DESIGNER: LAURA HOWARD

WHAT YOU NEED

(for each cake topper)

Templates (page 116)

Basic sewing kit (page 9)

Various bright contrasting colors of felt scraps:

- 1¾ x 1¾ inches (4.4 x 4.4 cm) of one color for the small circle (or other shape)

- 2 x 4 inches (5.1 x 10.2 cm) of a second color for the large circles

- 2½ x 2½ inches (6.4 x 6.4 cm) of a third color for the pinked edging

Embroidery floss and sewing thread to match the large circles

1 toothpick

WHAT YOU DO

1 For each cake topper, cut out one small circle (or heart, star, or flower) in one color and two large circles in a contrasting color. (The second large circle will go on the back of the cake topper.) If you're making a set of toppers to spell out a word or phrase, plan your arrangement before you start, to make sure the colors will be evenly spaced.

2 Pin one large circle to a piece of felt in a third contrasting color, then cut around the circle with pinking sheers to make a slightly larger circle with a zigzag edge.

3 Divide a six-strand length of embroidery floss that's the same color as the large circle into three strands. Place the small circle (or other small shape) in the center of the large circle, and place them on top of the pinked circle. Hold or pin the layers together, and backstitch through them with the floss and a large needle, inside the edge of the smallest shape.

4 If you're adding an initial to the cake topper, use more embroidery floss to backstitch the letter in the center of the small circle (leave the other small shapes undecorated).

5 Center the second large circle on the back of the cake topper, and sew it in place with the running stitch in matching color thread. Sew around the edge of the large circle, turning the cake topper back and forth as you sew to make sure your stitching doesn't overlap onto the small central shape. (Or cheat and just attach this back circle with fabric glue.) When stitching (or gluing) along this back circle's bottom, leave a small gap for a toothpick to fit through. Repeat all the steps to make as many cake toppers as desired, and add the toothpicks before you use them on your cake or cupcakes.

This cheerful felt gift bag will still be loved long after the party favors inside are gone.

Toadstool Gift Bag

DESIGNER: AMANDA CARESTIO

WHAT YOU NEED

Templates (page 115)

Basic sewing kit (page 9)

Fusible web

3 different polka dot fabrics, 3 x 3 inches (7.6 x 7.6 cm) each

3 squares of cream felt, 3 x 3 inches (7.6 x 7.6 cm) each

Blue felt, 21 x 18 inches (53.3 x 45.7 cm)

Tan and white thread

4 small grommets

24 inches (61 cm) of red cording

Heavy cardstock, 3 x 6 inches (7.6 x 15.2 cm) (optional)

WHAT YOU DO

1 Iron the fusible web to the back of the polka dot fabric squares. Trace the mushroom top templates onto the fusible-web side of these squares, and cut out the tops. Peel off the fusible web's paper backing.

2 Using the stem template, cut three stems from the cream squares of felt, varying the sizes as you go.

3 Cut the bag base from the blue felt, using the diagram (page 115) as a guide. Use pinking shears to cut the two 6-inch (15.2 cm) and two 3-inch (7.6 cm) outside edges (they'll form the top of the bag), and regular fabric scissors for the rest of the cuts.

4 On the front panel, pin and then stitch the stems in place, using the tan thread. Using a pressing cloth, iron the mushroom tops in place over the stems. Stitch in place with the white thread.

5 Pin the edges of the panels with wrong sides together and stitch with the white thread. Repeat for each side edge of the bag.

6 Set the grommets in the front and back bag panels, about ½ inch (1.3 cm) down from the top edge. Cut two 12-inch (30.5 cm) strands of cording. Thread each end through a grommet and knot on the inside of the bag.

Note: Place a 3 x 6-inch (7.6 x 15.2 cm) piece of heavy cardstock in the bottom of the bag for added strength and structure.

This easy-to-sew mobile would make a delightful addition to any nursery.

Flutterby Mobile

DESIGNER: LAURA HOWARD

WHAT YOU NEED

Template (page 117)

Basic sewing kit (page 9)

6 felt sheets of various colors, 9 x 12 inches (22.9 x 30.5 cm) each

Matching thread

About 6½ yards (5.9 m) of white yarn

The inner circle of a 7-inch (18 cm) embroidery hoop

WHAT YOU DO

1 Each shape in the mobile is made up of two identical pieces sewn together. To make the 12 butterflies and 12 circles, cut out 48 pieces in total: four butterfly shapes and four circle shapes from each of the six colors used. If you're using sturdy wool felt that won't flop, you can cut just one layer for each shape in the mobile, and skip the next step.

2 Align and pin one matching pair of shapes (wrong sides together if your felt seems to have a wrong side), and sew them together by using the running stitch and matching thread around the edge. Trim any excess felt to make sure the edges match up neatly.

3 Plan the arrangement of your mobile by spreading the shapes out on a flat surface to create four strands roughly even in length. Alternate between butterflies and circles, making sure the colors are spread evenly across the mobile.

4 Cut the white yarn to about 60 inches (1.5 m) in length, and knot it at one end. Using a large needle, sew one strand of the mobile together in the order you've arranged. Sew one long stitch through each

circle and about three stitches through each butterfly. Leave enough room between them on the yarn to allow all the pieces to spin easily, and leave plenty of yarn at the end for attaching to the hoop and hanging. Repeat this step for the remaining three strands.

Tip: If you like, you can paint the inner circle of the embroidery hoop white or any color to match your mobile before proceeding to the next step.

5 Wind the excess yarn of one strand around the inner circle of the embroidery hoop, adjusting it so the strand hangs at the desired height. Knot the yarn a couple of times to secure it in place. Don't trim the excess yarn yet! Repeat this for the other three strands, knotting them in place on the hoop as if they were the four points of a compass.

6 Hold all four yarn ends in your hand, so the hoop hangs level, and knot strands together. Use these strands to hang the mobile, then trim excess yarn once the mobile is in place. Hang it out of direct sunlight to avoid fading, and well out of the reach of babies and small children.

These adorable booties,
sewn from felted wool,
are sure to bring lots of
aaaahs at a baby shower.

Soft Baby Booties

DESIGNER: CYNTHIA SHAFFER

WHAT YOU NEED

Templates (page 113)

Basic sewing kit (page 9)

Fusible knit interfacing, ¼ yard (.2 m)

Felted garment wool, 12 x 12 inches (30.5 x 30.5 cm)

Felted garment wool in a coordinating color, 12 x 12 inches (30.5 x 30.5 cm)

Mocha brown embroidery floss

2 small sew-on snaps

2 pearl beads

WHAT YOU DO

1 Fuse the interfacing to the back of both pieces of felt.

2 Fold the felt for the top of the booties right sides together. Using templates A and B, cut out one pair for each template. Fold the felt for the soles of the booties right sides together. Use template C to cut out one pair of soles. Using the templates as a guide, mark the front notches and the notch at the heels.

3 To begin making one bootie, place the two upper shoe parts right sides together at the center back and stitch together using a ⅜-inch (.95 cm) seam allowance. Press the center back seam open, and then stitch the seam allowance down, ¼ inch (6 mm) from the seam.

4 Use the mocha brown embroidery floss to stitch a blanket stitch around the inside edge of the upper bootie.

5 Overlap the upper bootie at the toe, matching the center front notches, and machine baste together.

6 Pin the sole to the upper bootie, right sides together, and stitch using a ⅜-inch (.95 cm) seam allowance. Trim the seam allowance down to ¼ inch (6 mm), and turn the bootie right side out.

7 Sew a small snap to the underside of the strap and to the outside of the bootie where indicated on the template.

8 Use the template to cut a flower from the coordinating felt. Cut a small circle from the felt used for the upper shoe, and hand stitch a blanket stitch around the circle's perimeter with the mocha brown floss. Stitch the small circle to the inside portion of the flower and then to the end of the shoe strap. Be certain these are attached very securely. Sew a small coordinating pearl bead very securely to the inside of the flower. Repeat steps 3 through 8 to make the second bootie, but in step 5, overlap the upper bootie in the opposite direction from the first bootie.

TEMPLATES

For information on enlarging and transferring templates, see Using Templates on page 9.

For information on enlarging and transferring templates, see Using Templates on page 9.

April Showers
Page 46—copy at 100%

Apple for Teacher Brooch
Page 50—copy at 100%

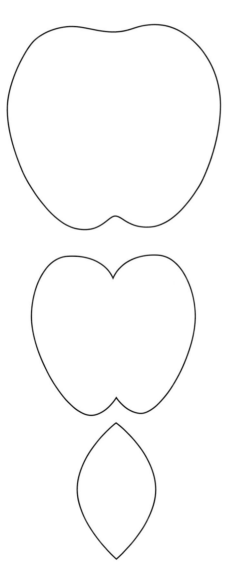

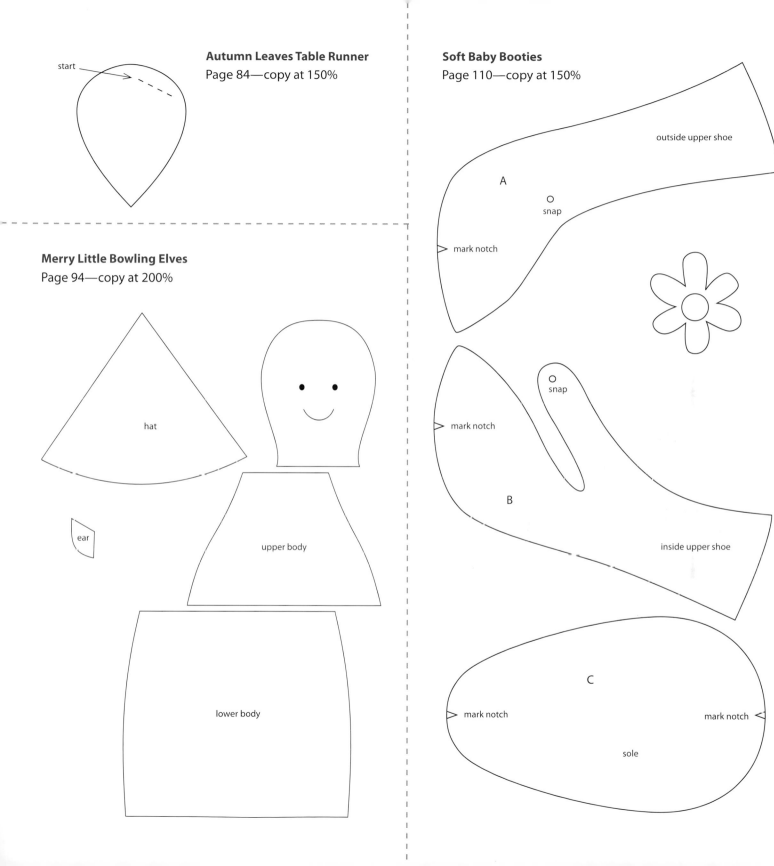

Autumn Leaves Table Runner
Page 84—copy at 150%

start

Soft Baby Booties
Page 110—copy at 150%

outside upper shoe

A

snap

mark notch

Merry Little Bowling Elves
Page 94—copy at 200%

hat

ear

upper body

lower body

mark notch

snap

B

inside upper shoe

C

mark notch

mark notch

sole

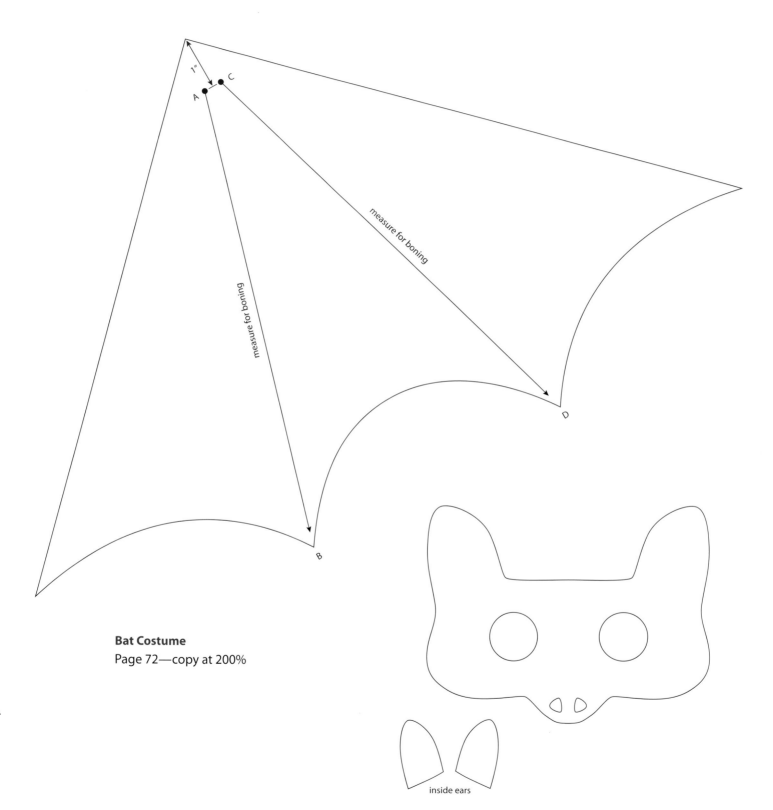

1"

A

C

measure for boning

measure for boning

B

D

Bat Costume
Page 72—copy at 200%

inside ears

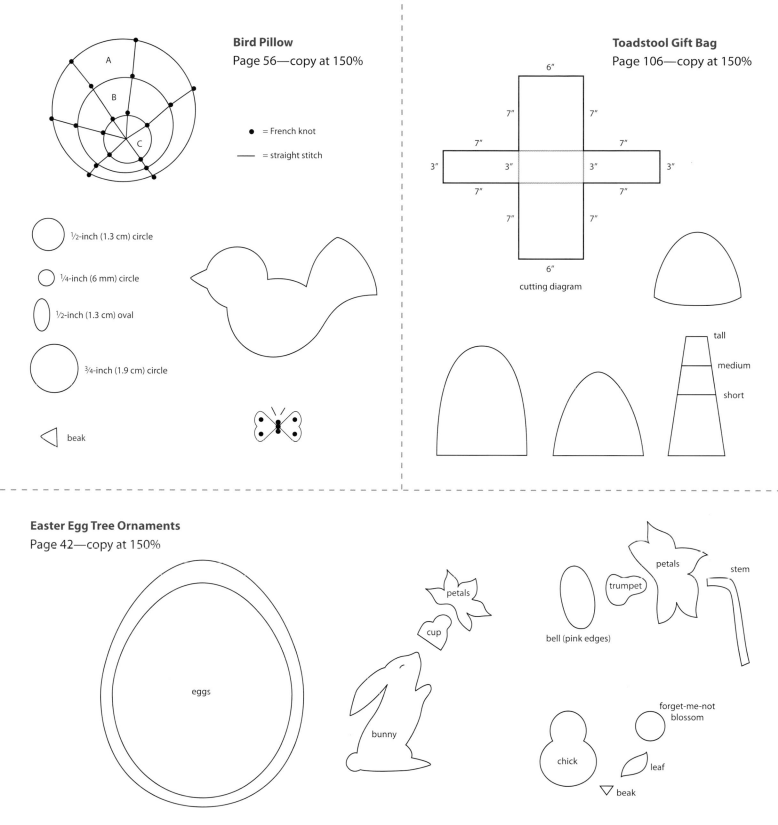

Bird Pillow
Page 56—copy at 150%

A

B

C

• = French knot

— = straight stitch

½-inch (1.3 cm) circle

¼-inch (6 mm) circle

½-inch (1.3 cm) oval

¾-inch (1.9 cm) circle

beak

Toadstool Gift Bag
Page 106—copy at 150%

6"

7"   7"

7"   7"

3"   3"   3"   3"

7"   7"

7"   7"

6"

cutting diagram

tall

medium

short

Easter Egg Tree Ornaments
Page 42—copy at 150%

eggs

petals

cup

bunny

petals

trumpet   stem

bell (pink edges)

forget-me-not
blossom

chick   leaf

beak

Bunny Pal

Page 38—copy at 300%

eye   pupil

(also use for egg dots)

leg

arm

ear

body

arm here   arm here

A   B

egg

head piece

Cake Toppers

Page 103—copy at 125%

HAPPY BIRTHDAY

Seeing Shadows Phone Case
Page 24—copy at 200%

body

shadow

Halloweenie Bag
Page 75—copy at 150%

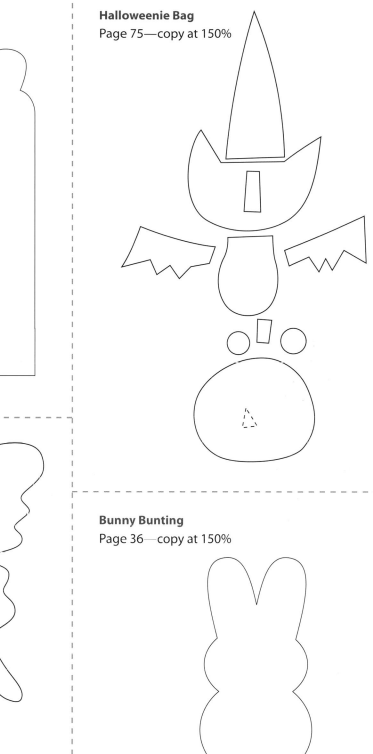

Flutterby Mobile
Page 108—copy at 150%

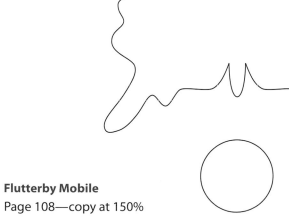

Bunny Bunting
Page 36—copy at 150%

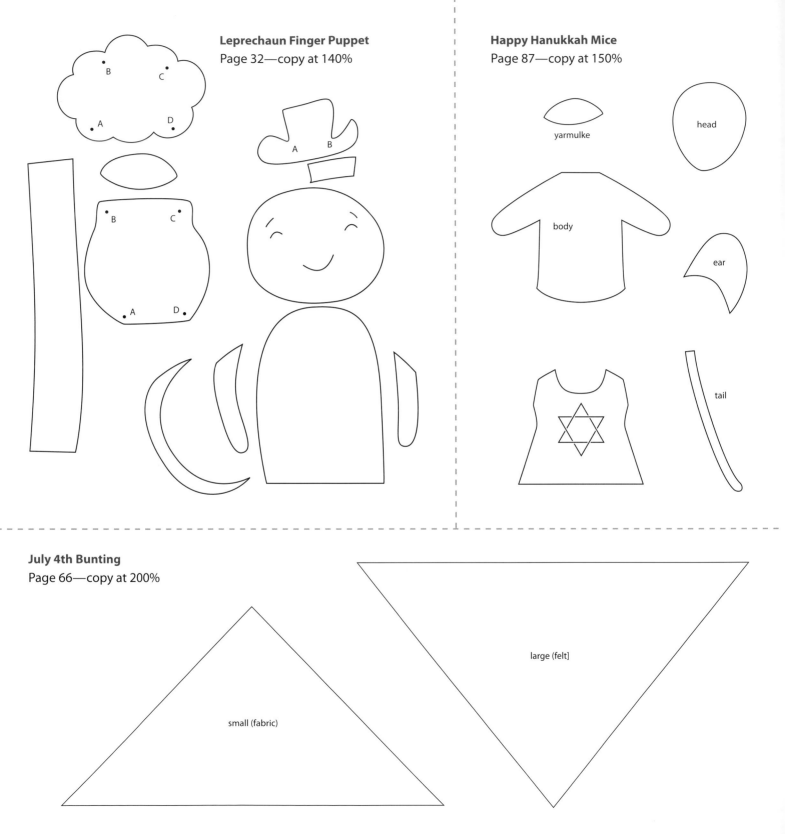

Leprechaun Finger Puppet
Page 32—copy at 140%

Happy Hanukkah Mice
Page 87—copy at 150%

yarmulke

head

body

ear

tail

July 4th Bunting
Page 66—copy at 200%

large (felt)

small (fabric)

Cheers! Banner
Page 14—copy at 200%

I Have a Dream Garland
Page 20—copy at 100%

CHERS
!

Happy Birthday Crown
Page 100—copy at 250%

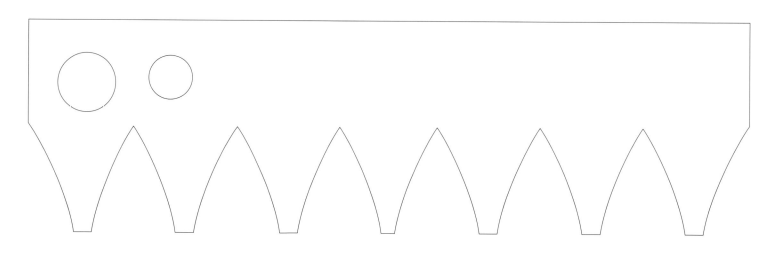

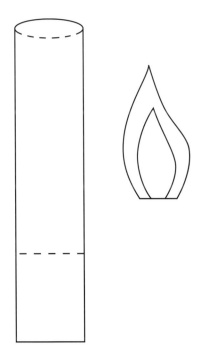

Kwanzaa Kinara
Page 97—copy at 110%

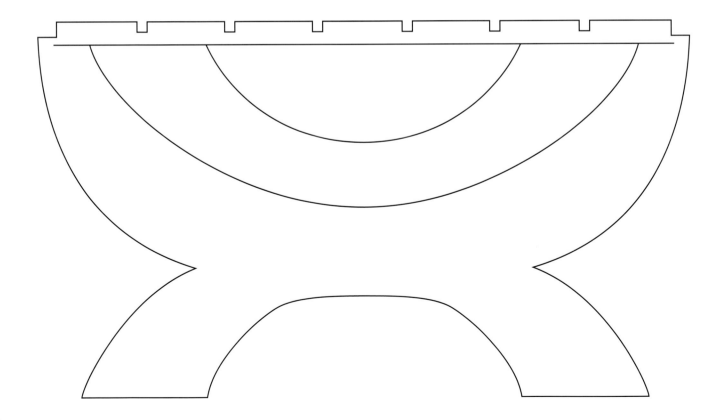

Heart-Felt Holidays

Earth Day Leaf Garlands
Page 44—copy at 100%

Autumn Leaves Coasters
Page 82—copy at 100%

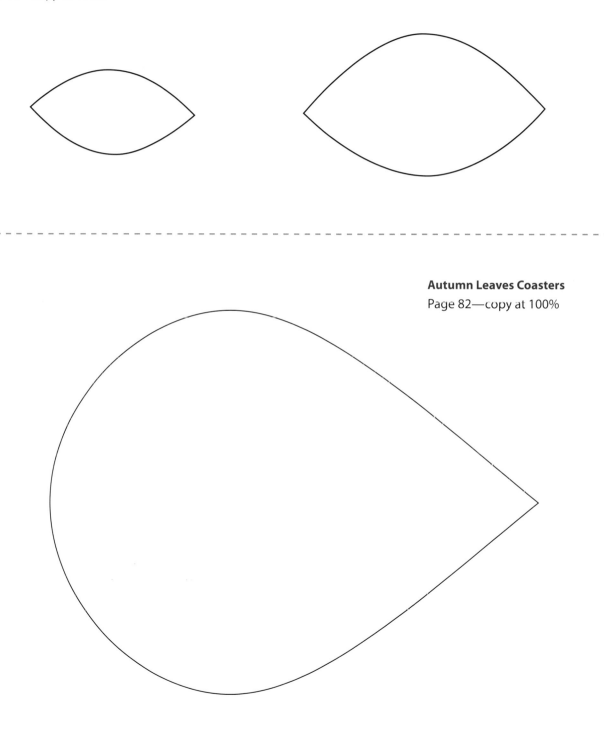

The Great Mini Pumpkins
Page 78—copy at 100%

leaf

pumpkin body panel

Piñata Ornaments
Page 52—copy at 100%

Manly Moustaches
Page 62—copy at 100%

outer moustache

inner moustache

Felt Mistletoe Kissing Ball
Page 92—copy at 100%

center

petal

fold

Lavender Tea Bag Sachets
Page 54—copy at 100%

May Flowers Garland
Page 48—copy at 100%

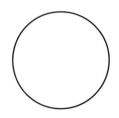

Christmas Ornaments
Page 90—copy at 100%

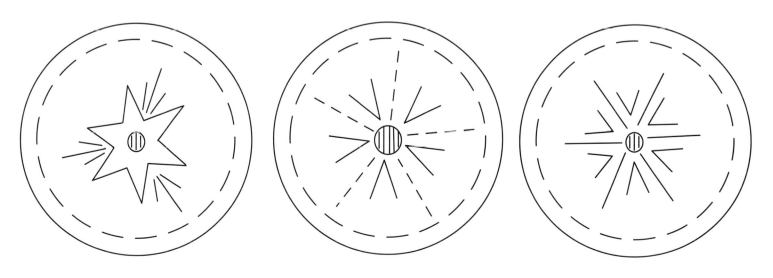

Yo Ho Ho Pirate Parrot
Page 68—copy at 200%

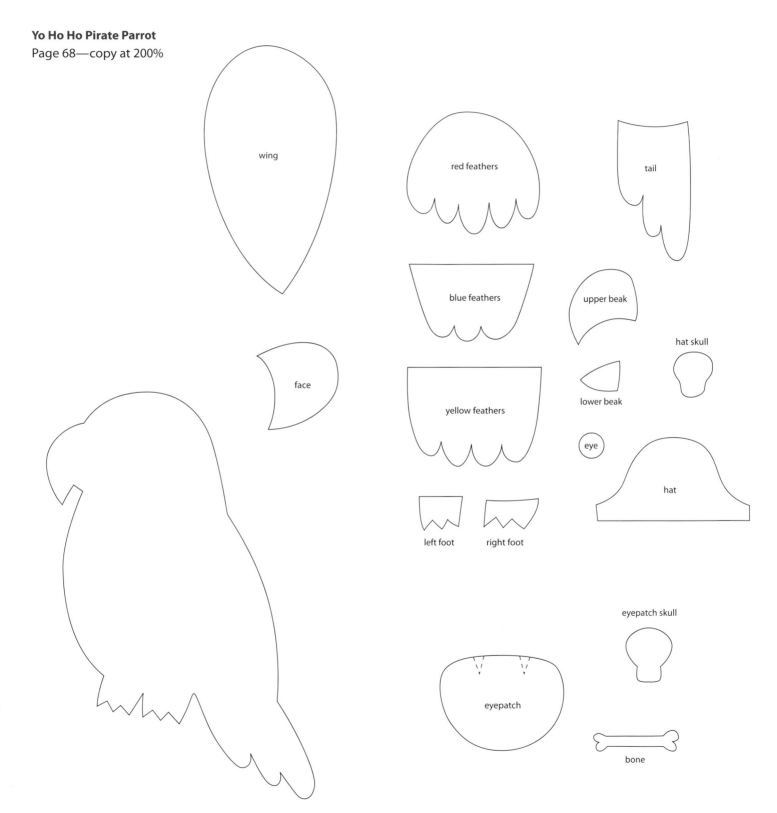

wing

red feathers

tail

blue feathers

upper beak

hat skull

face

lower beak

yellow feathers

eye

hat

left foot

right foot

eyepatch skull

eyepatch

bone

Mushroom Love Brooch
Page 26—copy at 100%

Heart Baubles
Page 30—copy at 150%

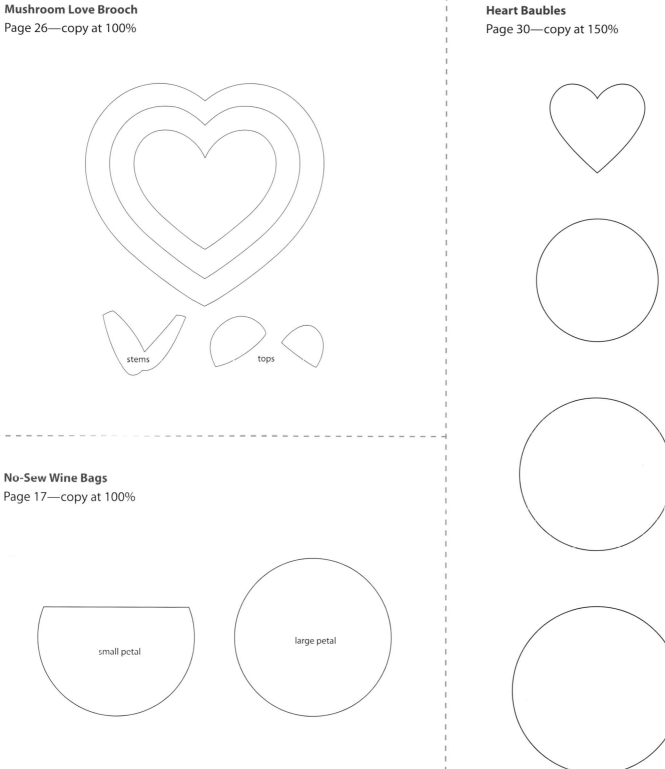

stems

tops

No-Sew Wine Bags
Page 17—copy at 100%

small petal

large petal

Felty Family Portraits

Page 60—copy at 130%

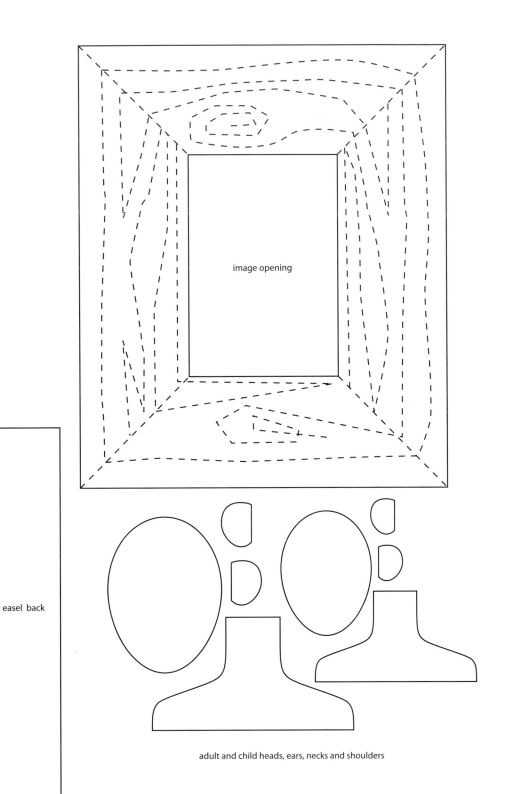

image opening

easel back

fold back

adult and child heads, ears, necks and shoulders

Blooming Valentines
Page 28—copy at 100%

(Pumpkin) Pie in the Sky
Page 80—copy at 120%

whipped cream

top/bottom

crust

side piece

Chinese Luck Lantern

Page 22—copy at 110%

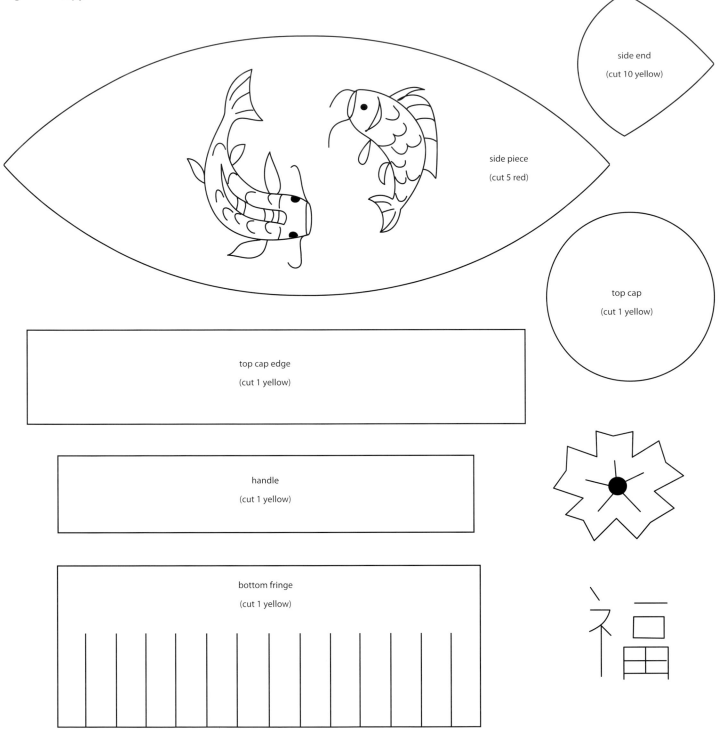

side end
(cut 10 yellow)

side piece
(cut 5 red)

top cap
(cut 1 yellow)

top cap edge
(cut 1 yellow)

handle
(cut 1 yellow)

bottom fringe
(cut 1 yellow)

福

ABOUT *the* DESIGNERS

ELLEN LUCKETT BAKER

Ellen Luckett Baker is the author of *1,2,3 Sew* from Chronicle Books. She also writes the blog The Long Thread (www.thelongthread.com), where she shares craft and sewing tutorials. Ellen lives in Atlanta, Georgia, with her husband and two daughters.

CONSTANÇA CABRAL

Born and raised in Lisbon, Portugal, Constança Cabral now spends her days amongst fabrics in her home studio facing an ever-changing garden in Staffordshire, England. A self-taught seamstress and a firm believer in handmade goods and seasonal living, she creates unique pieces for women and children alike. You can her find daily at www.saidosdaconcha.blogspot.com.

REBEKAH J. CHAMBERLIN

A self-proclaimed "feltaholic," Rebekah J. Chamberlin is constantly crafting and designing with user-friendly felt products in mind. Most of her designs center around bright colors in modern designs with a bit of whimsy. Her claim to felt fame is her non-traditional Christmas stockings that appear to have come to life right out of your favorite storybook. View her designs and products at her Etsy shop MissMosh (www.etsy.com/shop/missmosh).

CATHY GAUBERT

Cathy Gaubert is a wife, momma, maker of things, and the author of *Pretty in Patchwork: Doll Quilts* from Lark Crafts. Her days are filled with the antics of three sweet girlies, and her kitchen table is filled with more works in progress than you can shake a stick at. Peer into her world at www.handmadecathygaubert.blogspot.com, and do be sure to say hello.

LAURA HOWARD

Laura "Lupin" Howard is a not quite grown up girl living in Gloucester, England, who likes to make and do. She drinks a lot of tea, is partial to a nice bit of cake, and is completely obsessed with felt. Much of her work is inspired by English country gardens, native British wildlife, and the vibrant colors of felt in her stash. When she's not busy sewing, she designs tutorials for books and magazines and writes about her crafty exploits on her blog, www.bugsandfishes.blogspot.com. Laura has been selling her hand-stitched felt crafts online since 2007 and can be contacted via her website, www.lupinhandmade.com.

MOLLIE JOHANSON

Mollie Johanson, a trained graphic designer specializing in print projects, began her blog, Wild Olive (www.wildolive.blogspot.com), as an outlet for more whimsical works. Daily dreaming and doodling have resulted in a variety of embroidery and paper projects, most featuring simple expressive faces. Mollie, based in a far western suburb of Chicago, commutes daily to her in-home studio via the coffee pot.

LISA JORDAN

Lisa Jordan is an artist deeply inspired by nature. Whether working with felted sweaters or lumps of wood, the imprint of her natural surroundings in rural Minnesota are evident in her work. When she's not crafting, she blogs about her life under the poplar and pine at www.lilfishstudios.com.

ABOUT *the* DESIGNERS (continued)

STEPHANIE LYNN LIEBERT

Stephanie Lynn Liebert has a passion for do-it-yourself décor, home projects, and anything that keeps her creative mind busy. She enjoys the challenge of designing projects on her own; preferably using repurposed items when possible. Her blog, www.bystephanielynn.com, is dedicated to inspiring others to find their inner creativity by sharing a variety of simple projects, fun crafts, and occasional recipes.

SUZIE MILLIONS

Suzie Millions is an artist and compulsive crafter living in Asheville, North Carolina. Her book, *The Complete Book of Retro Crafts*, was published by Lark Crafts in 2009, and her wonderfully quirky work has appeared in numerous other books by Lark. To see more of her art, visit her website www.suziemillions.com.

AIMEE RAY

Aimee Ray has been making things from paper, fabric, and clay for as long as she can remember. She has a head full of ideas and is always working on something new. She is the author of *Doodle-Stitching* and *Doodle-Stitching: The Motif Collection*, two books of contemporary embroidery designs, and has contributed to many other Lark Crafts titles. You can see more of her work at www.dreamfollow.com.

CYNTHIA SHAFFER

Cynthia Shaffer is a quilter and creative sewer whose love of fabric can be traced back to the age of six, when she learned to sew and in no time was designing and sewing clothing for herself and others. After earning a degree in textiles, Cynthia worked for 10 years as the owner of a company that specialized in the design and manufacture of sportswear. Numerous books and magazines have featured Cynthia's art and photography work: she is the author of *Stash Happy Patchwork* (Lark, 2011) and *Stash Happy Appliqué* (Lark, 2012). For more information visit her online at www.cynthiashaffer.com or www.cynthiashaffer.typepad.com.

DANA WILLARD

Dana Willard is author of the book, *The Fabric Selector: The Essential Guide to Working with Fabrics, Trimmings, and Notions*, and she authors the popular DIY sewing design blog MADE (www.dana-made-it.com). Her eye-catching photography and easy-to-follow tutorials with fresh sewing patterns and techniques have attracted many followers. Dana's designs have been featured in various sewing books, publications, and online communities. She lives in the hot city of Austin, Texas, with her husband and two kids.

CATHY ZIEGELE

Cathy Ziegele, motivated by a scandalously naked troll doll, sewed her first felt caveman garment at age six. Her love of sewing grew from there. A retired executive chef, Cathy finds the ease of working with felt to be a nice departure from the chopping and dicing required when working with food. Cathy's pincushions are available for purchase online at www.thedailypincushion.etsy.com.

Acknowledgments

We simply could not do what we do without our incredibly talented and hardworking designers. They make the work of putting together a book a pleasure and continue to inspire us. Be sure to read about them, starting on page 129, and visit their blogs and shops.

Thanks to Alpha Mom (www.alphamom.com) for allowing us to share Ellen Luckett Baker's Bat Costume. And thanks to Brenda Ponnay (www.secret-agent-josephine.com/blog), whose paper confetti popper rockets inspired our felt rockets.

Thanks to Kay Holmes Stafford for putting all the words and pictures together to make a beautiful book.

The first question we asked when deciding whether or not to do another felt book was, Will Susan Wasinger photograph and design it? We're so glad she said yes.

About the Authors

Kathy Sheldon currently writes, edits, and packages craft books while dividing her time between Asheville, North Carolina; Charleston, South Carolina; and Windham, Maine. She used to write books on gardening and outdoor living, but moved inside to craft when the bugs got too bad. The development editor for *Fa la la la Felt*, she has recently pushed the felt and floss aside on her craft table to make room for shrink plastic jewelry.

Amanda Carestio's latest crafting obsessions are mini quilts and furniture makeovers. When she's not bent over her sewing machine or exploring the Blue Ridge Mountains, Amanda enjoys spending quality time with her hubby and super-spoiled canines in Asheville, North Carolina. The head of Lark's Needlearts team, she is the author of *Fa La La La Felt* and *Stash Happy: Felt*. Her designs appear in several other Lark books; she blogs online at www.larkcrafts.com and at www.digsandbean.blogspot.com.

Index

Backstitch, 11

Basics, 6

Blanket stitch, 11

Celebrations,

    Birthday, 100, 103, 106

    Baby Shower, 108, 110

Double-threaded running stitch, 12

Embellishments, 8

Felting sweaters, 8

Finishing edges, 10

Free-motion sewing, 10

French knot, 12

Floss, 8

Holidays,

    Cinco de Mayo, 52

    Chinese New Year, 22

    Christmas, 90, 92, 94

    Earth Day, 44

Easter, 36, 38, 42

Father's Day, 59, 62

Fourth of July, 64, 66

Groundhog Day, 24

Halloween, 72, 75, 78

Hanukkah, 87

Kwanzaa, 97

Martin Luther King Day, 20

May Day, 48

Mother's Day, 54, 56

New Year's, 14, 16

Spring Showers, 46

St. Patrick's Day, 32

Teacher Appreciation Day, 50

Thanksgiving, 80, 82, 84

Talk Like a Pirate Day, 68

Valentine's Day, 26, 28, 30

Lazy daisy stitch, 11

No-sew projects, 16, 48, 64, 92, 98

Running stitch, 12

Satin Stitch, 11

Sewing kit, 9

Single-threaded running stitch, 12

Split stitch, 12

Stem stitch, 12

Templates, 9, 112

Thread, 8

Types of felt,

    Acrylic, 8

    Bamboo, 8

    Eco, 8

    Wool, 7

    Wool/rayon, 7

Whipstitch, 11